EASY PIANO

FIRST 50
CHRISTMAS CAROLS

YOU SHOULD PLAY ON THE PIANO

ISBN 978-1-4950-2658-4

HAL•LEONARD®
CORPORATION
7777 W. BLUEMOUND RD. P.O. BOX 13819 MILWAUKEE, WI 53213

In Australia Contact:
Hal Leonard Australia Pty. Ltd.
4 Lentara Court
Cheltenham, Victoria, 3192 Australia
Email: ausadmin@halleonard.com.au

Visit Hal Leonard Online at
www.halleonard.com

CONTENTS

ANGELS FROM THE REALMS OF GLORY

Words by JAMES MONTGOMERY
Music by HENRY T. SMART

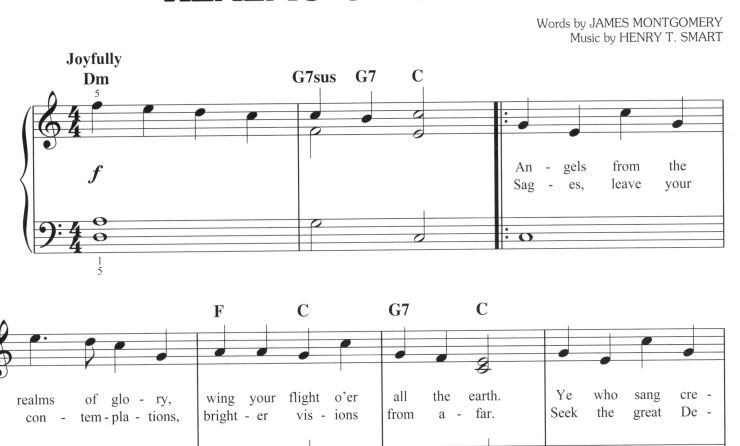

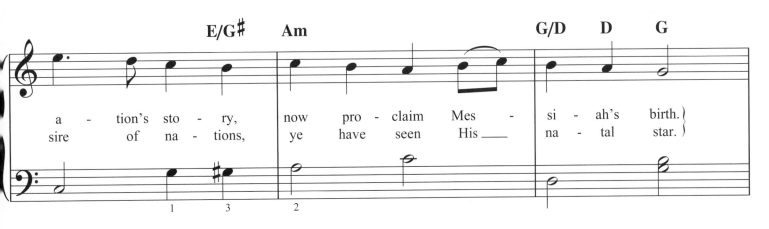

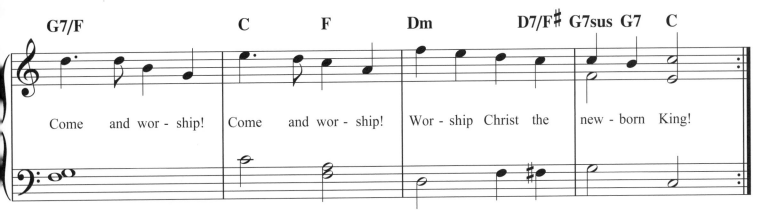

ANGELS WE HAVE HEARD ON HIGH

Traditional French Carol
Translated by JAMES CHADWICK

Moderately

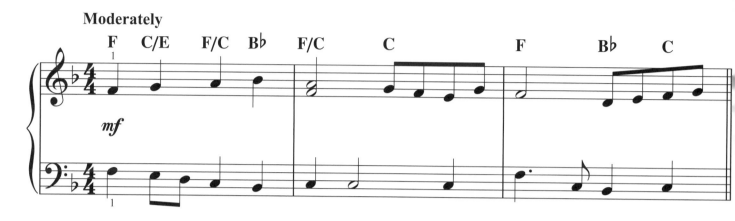

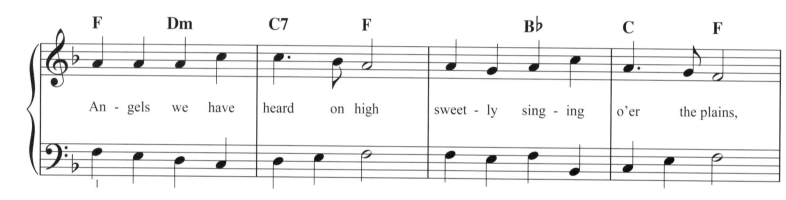

Angels we have heard on high sweet-ly sing-ing o'er the plains,

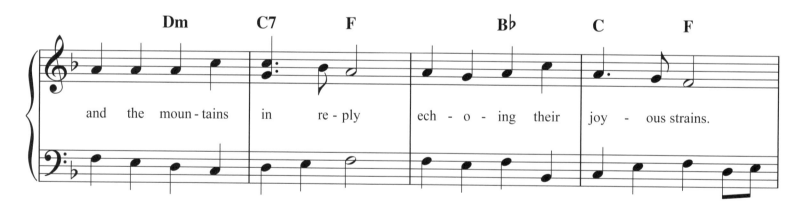

and the moun-tains in re-ply ech-o-ing their joy-ous strains.

Glo - - - - ri - a

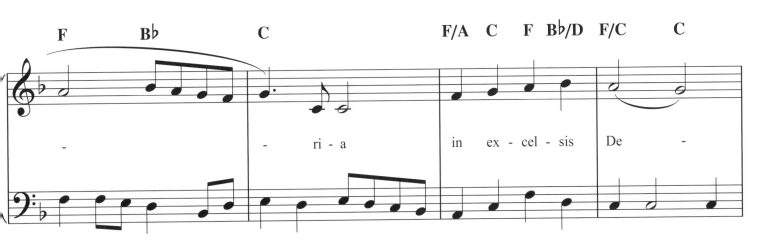

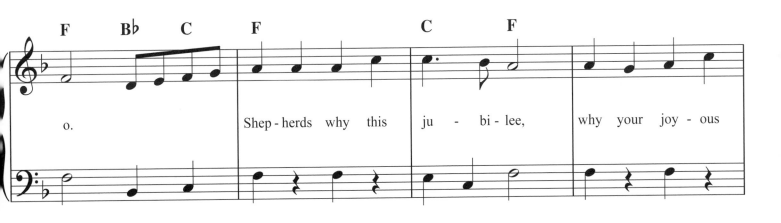

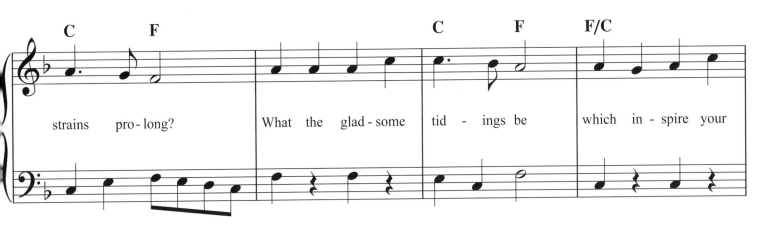

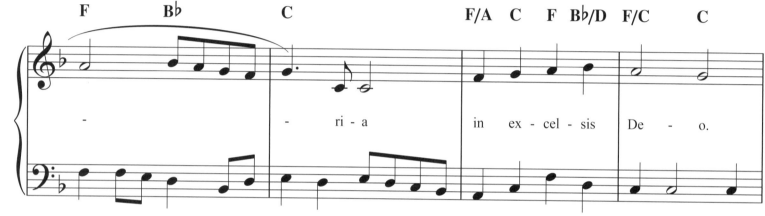

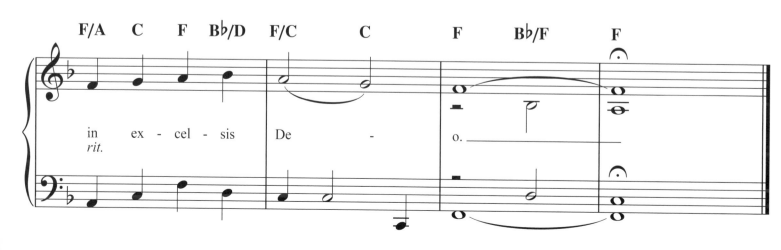

AS WITH GLADNESS MEN OF OLD

Words by WILLIAM CHATTERTON DIX
Music by CONRAD KOCHER

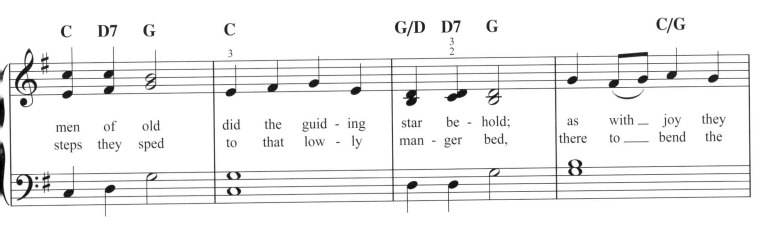

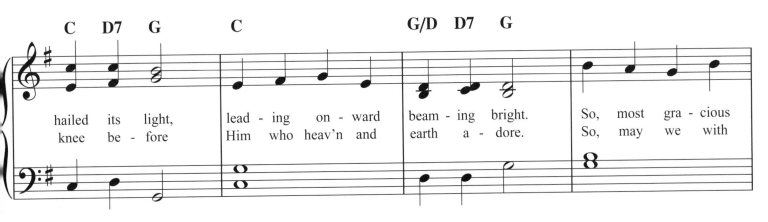

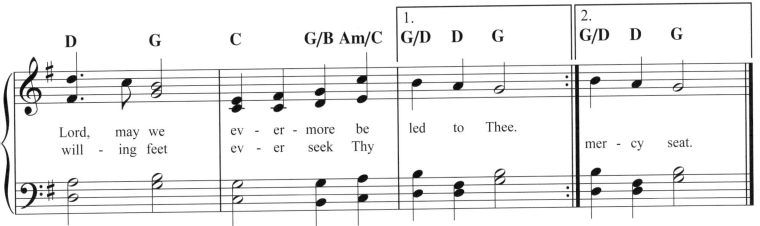

AULD LANG SYNE

Words by ROBERT BURNS
Traditional Scottish Melody

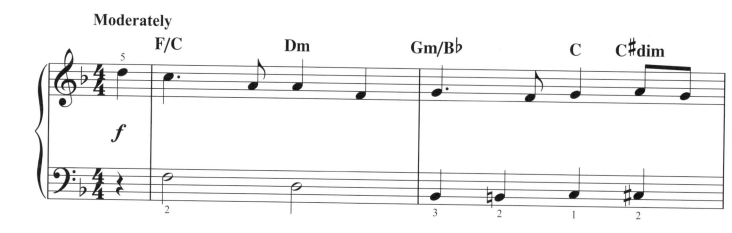

Should auld ac - quain - tance

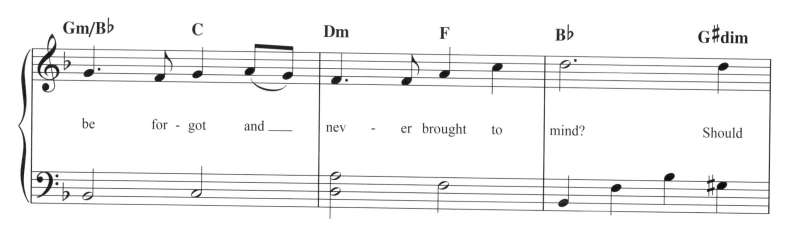

be for - got and ___ nev - er brought to mind? Should

9

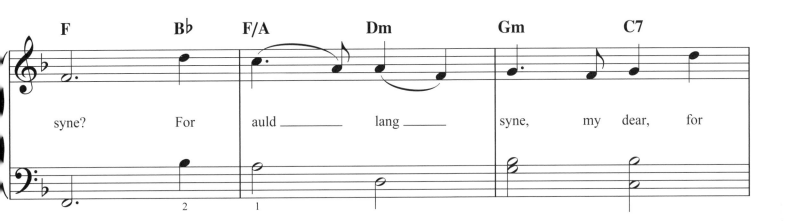

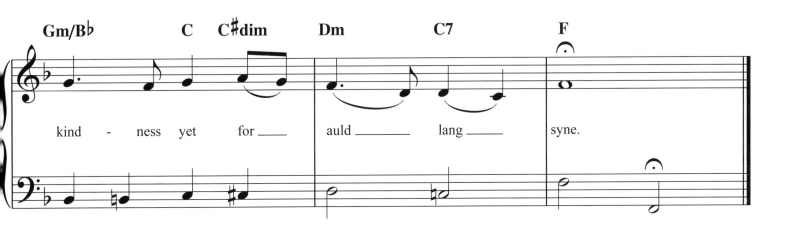

AWAY IN A MANGER

Words by JOHN T. McFARLAND (v.3)
Music by JAMES R. MURRAY

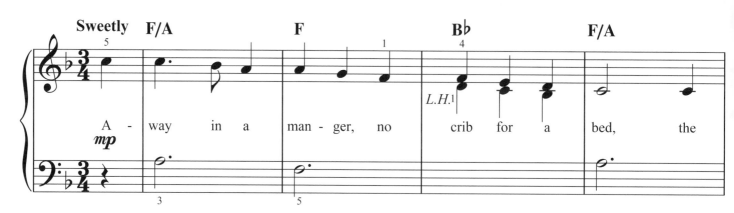

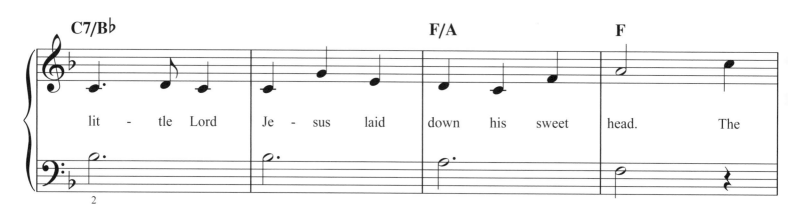

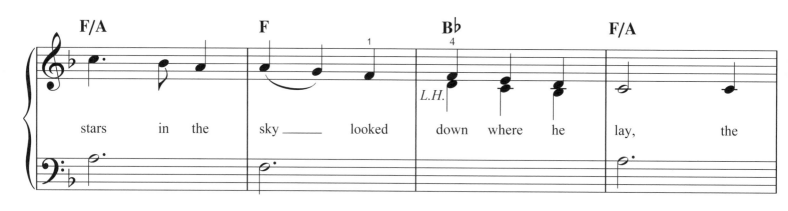

A CHILD IS BORN IN BETHLEHEM

14th-Century Latin Text adapted by NICOLAI F.S. GRUNDTVIG
Traditional Danish Melody

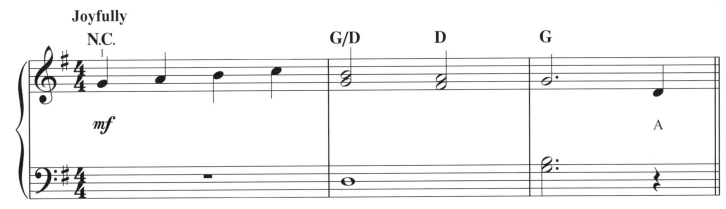

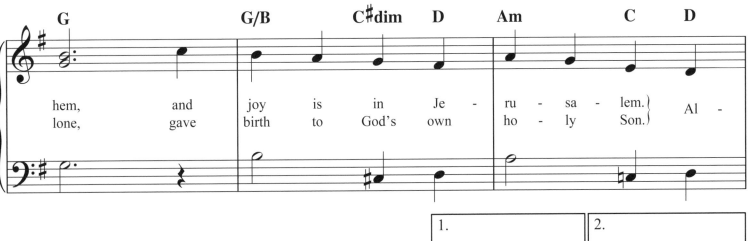

BRING A TORCH, JEANNETTE, ISABELLA

17th Century French Provençal Carol

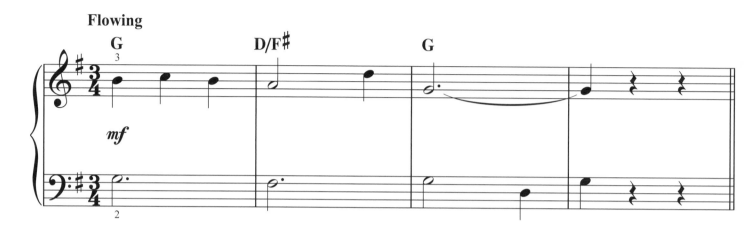

Bring a torch, ___ Jean - nette, Is - a - bel - la,
Has - ten now, ___ good folk of the vil - lage,

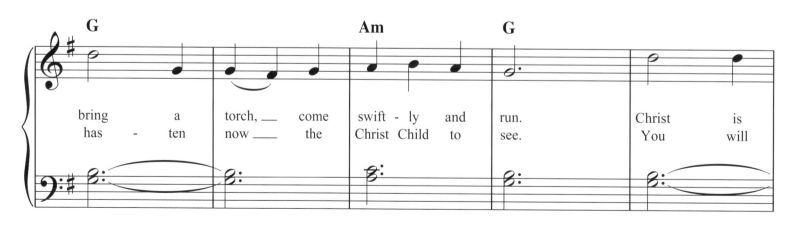

bring a torch, ___ come swift - ly and run.
has - ten now ___ the Christ Child to see.

Christ is
You will

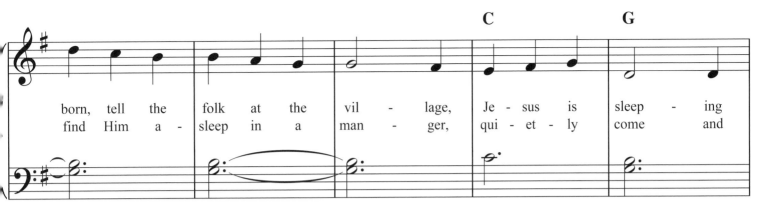

born, tell the | folk at the | vil - lage, | Je - sus is | sleep - ing
find Him a - | sleep in a | man - ger, | qui - et - ly | come and

in His | cra - dle. | Ah, _____ | ah, _____
whis - per | soft - ly. | Hush, _____ | hush, _____

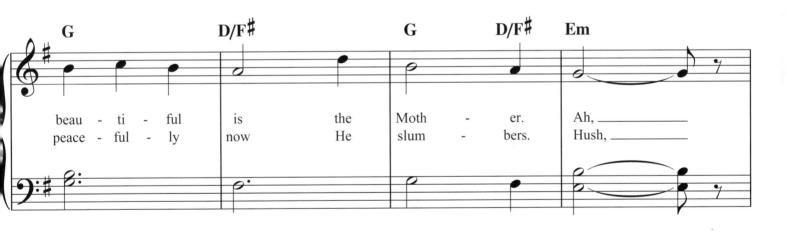

beau - ti - ful | is the | Moth - er. | Ah, _____
peace - ful - ly | now He | slum - bers. | Hush, _____

ah, _____ | beau - ti - ful | is her | Son. _____
hush, _____ | peace - ful - ly | now He | sleeps. _____

CANON IN D

By JOHANN PACHELBEL

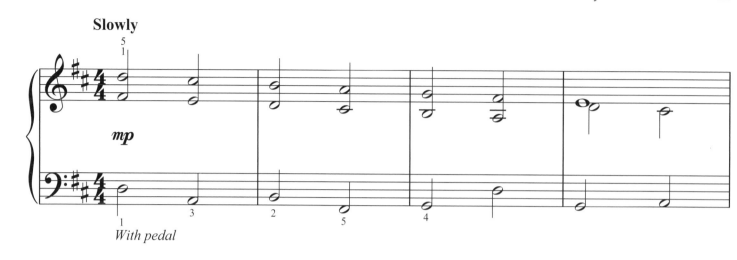

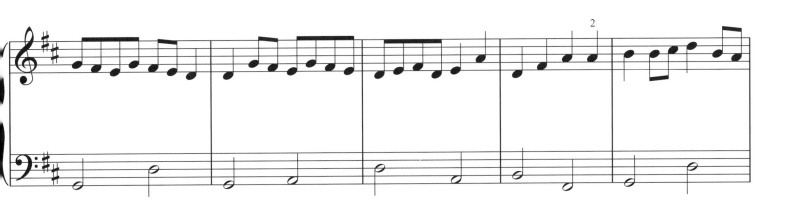

CHRIST WAS BORN ON CHRISTMAS DAY

Traditional

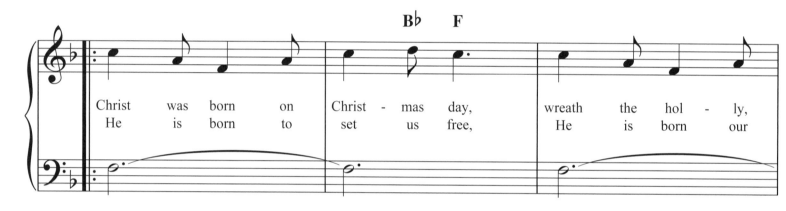

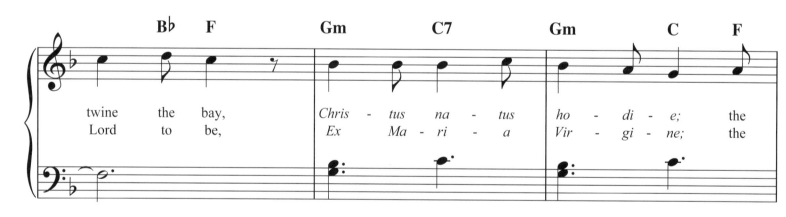

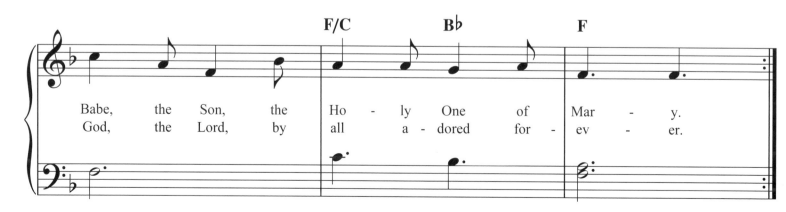

COVENTRY CAROL

Words by ROBERT CROO
Traditional English Melody

DECK THE HALL

Traditional Welsh Carol

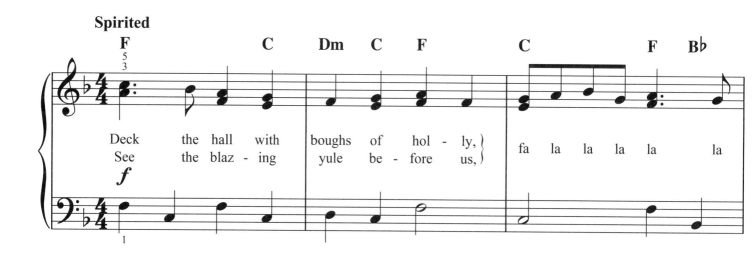

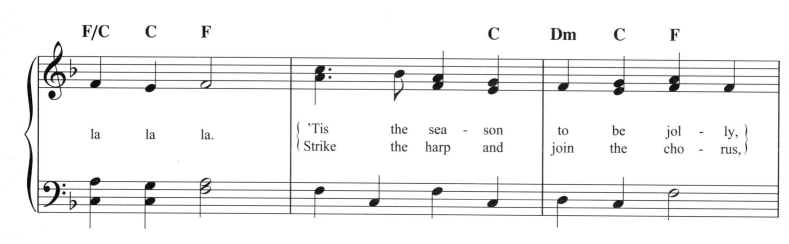

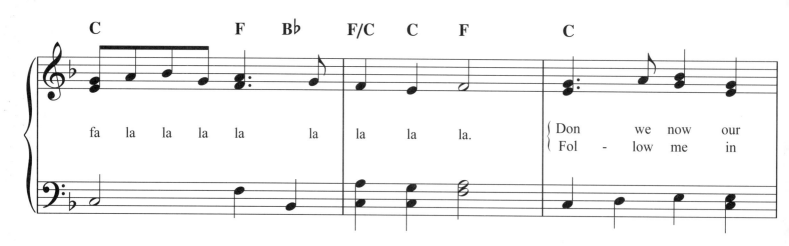

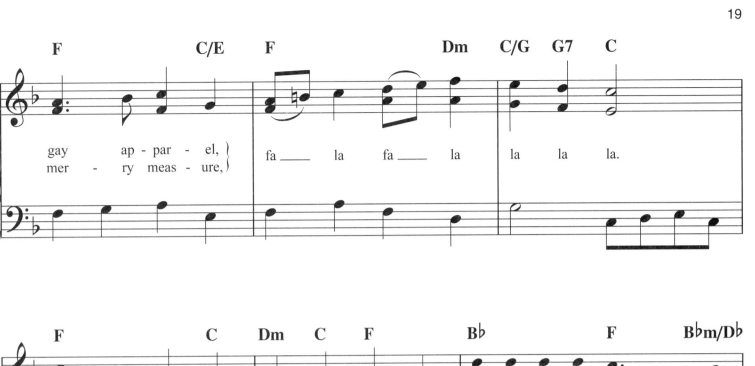

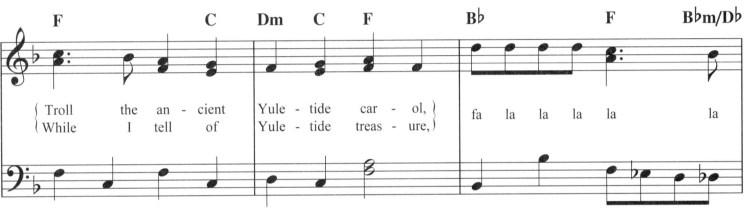

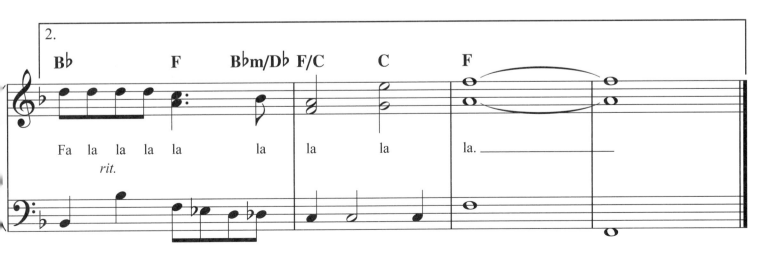

DING DONG! MERRILY ON HIGH!

French Carol

Moderately

Ding dong! Mer - ri - ly on high the
Ding dong! Car - ol all the bells, ring

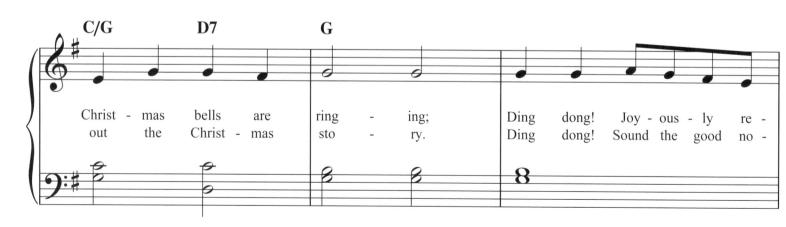

Christ - mas bells are ring - ing; Ding dong! Joy - ous - ly re -
out the Christ - mas sto - ry. Ding dong! Sound the good no -

THE FIRST NOËL

17th Century English Carol
Music from W. Sandys' *Christmas Carols*

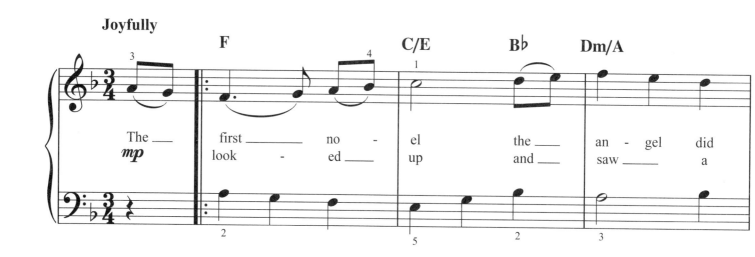

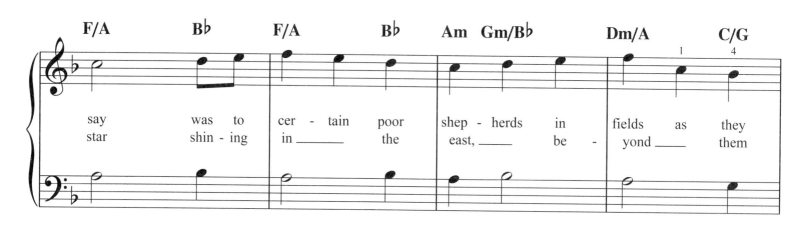

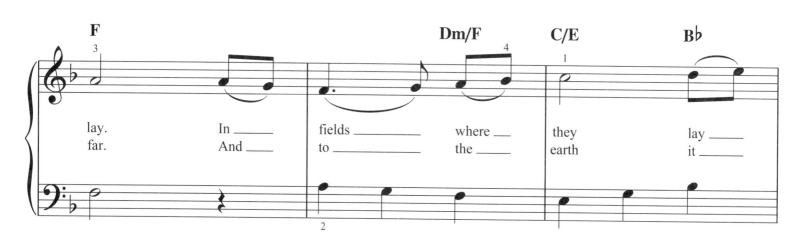

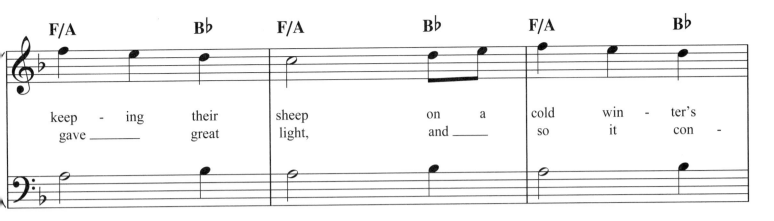

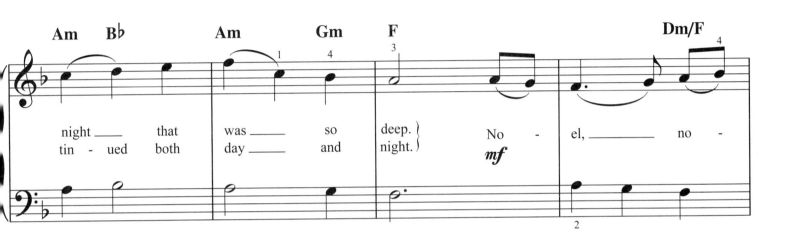

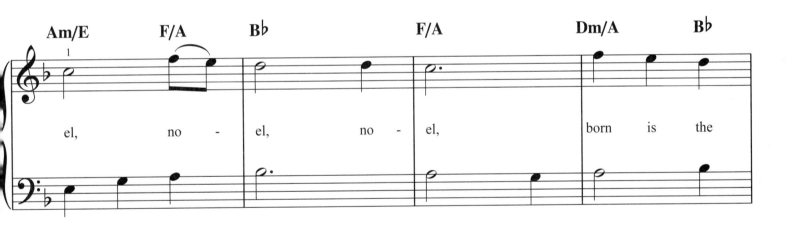

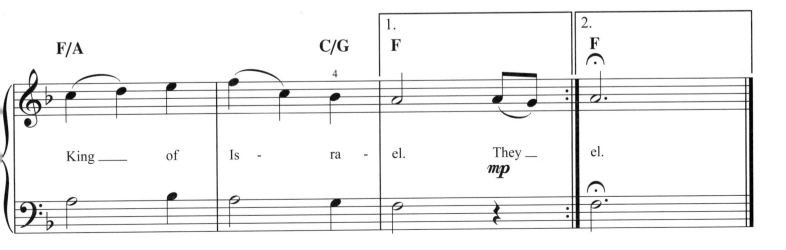

THE FRIENDLY BEASTS

Traditional English Carol

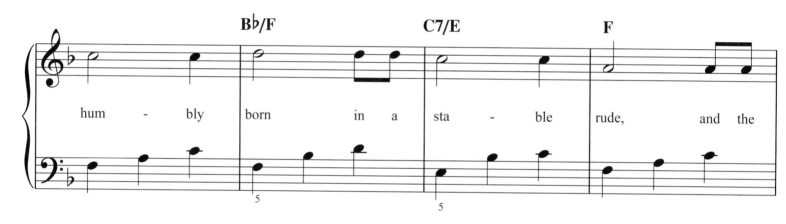

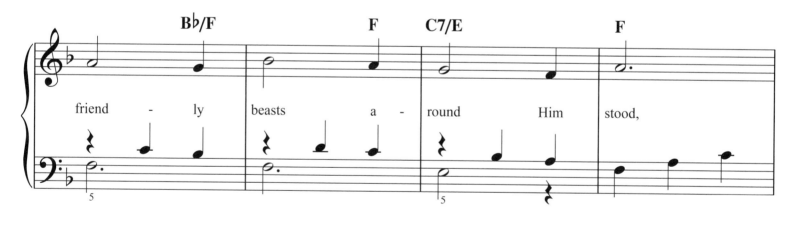

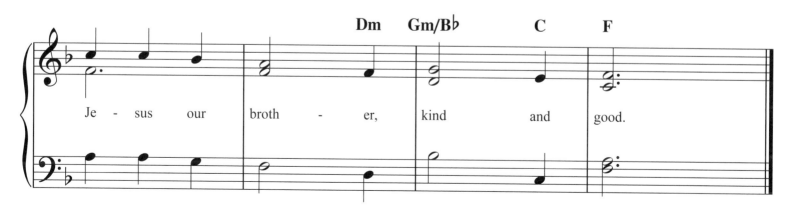

FUM, FUM, FUM

Traditional Catalonian Carol

GATHER AROUND
THE CHRISTMAS TREE

By JOHN H. HOPKINS

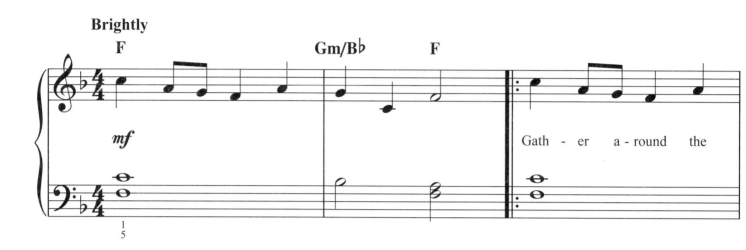

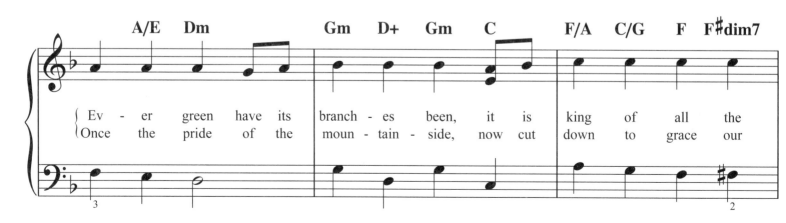

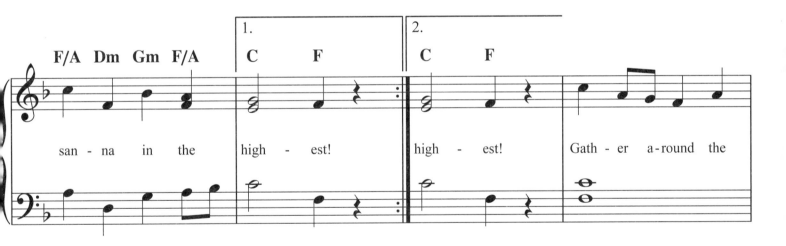

GO, TELL IT ON THE MOUNTAIN

African-American Spiritual
Verses by JOHN W. WORK, JR.

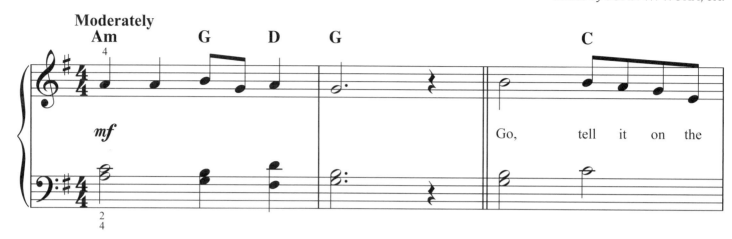

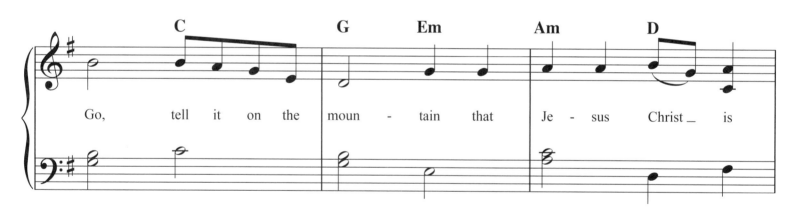

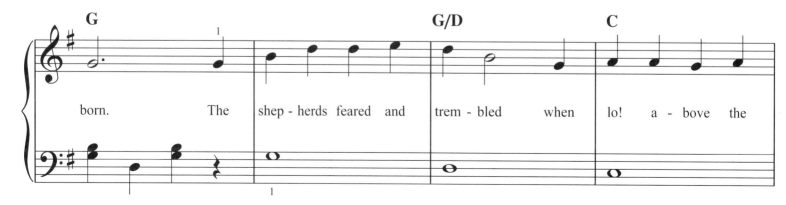

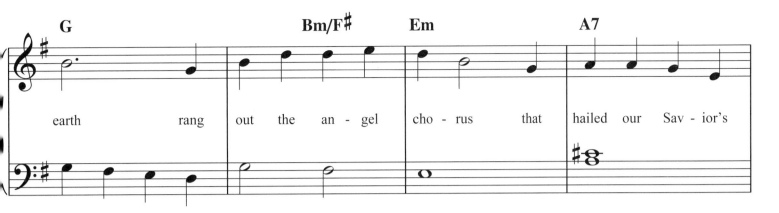

earth   rang   out the an - gel   cho - rus   that   hailed our Sav - ior's

birth. _____   Go,   tell it on the moun - tain,

o - ver the hills and   ev - 'ry - where.   Go,   tell it on the

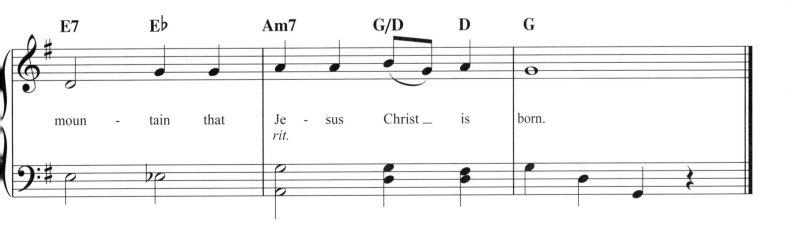

moun - tain that   Je - sus Christ _ is   born.

rit.

GOD REST YE MERRY, GENTLEMEN

19th Century English Carol

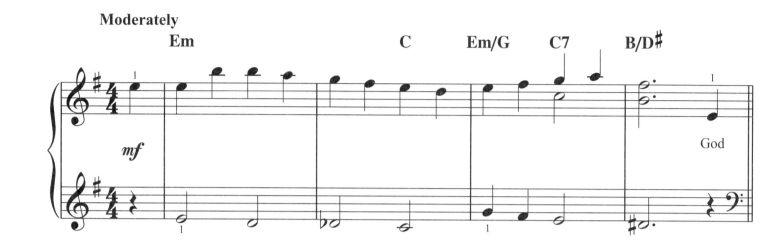

God

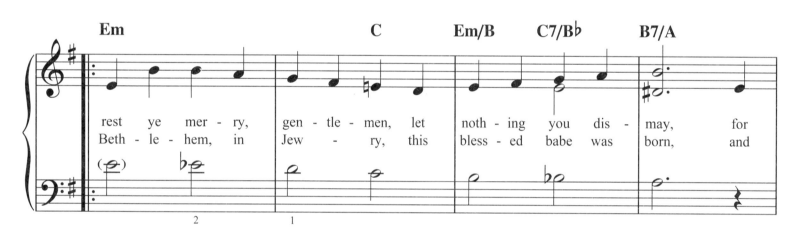

rest ye mer - ry, gen - tle - men, let noth - ing you dis - may, for
Beth - le - hem, in Jew - ry, this bless - ed babe was born, for and

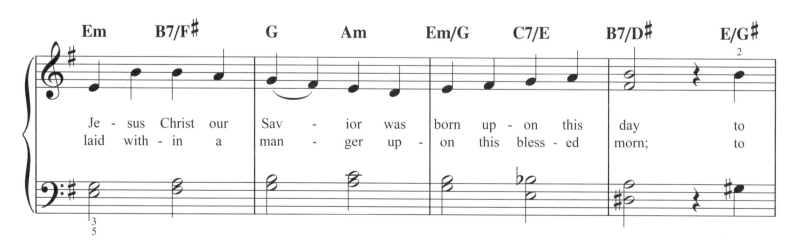

Je - sus Christ our Sav - ior was born up - on this day to
laid with - in a man - ger up - on this bless - ed morn; to

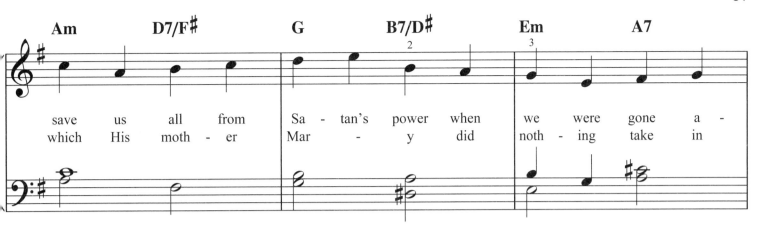

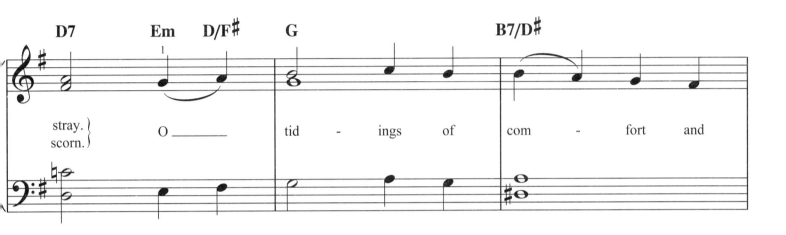

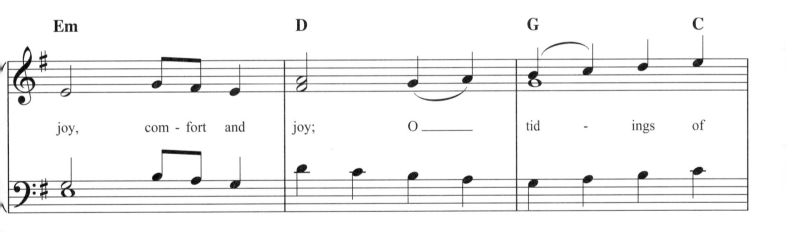

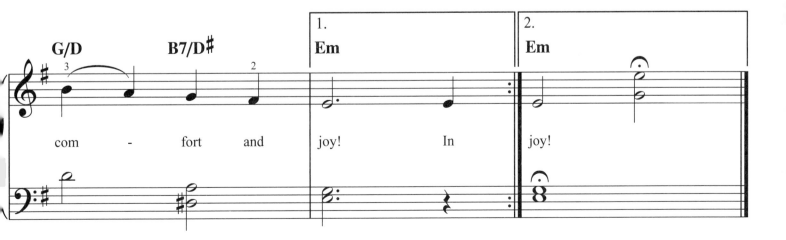

GOOD CHRISTIAN MEN, REJOICE

14th Century Latin Text
Translated by JOHN MASON NEALE
14th Century German Melody

With spirit

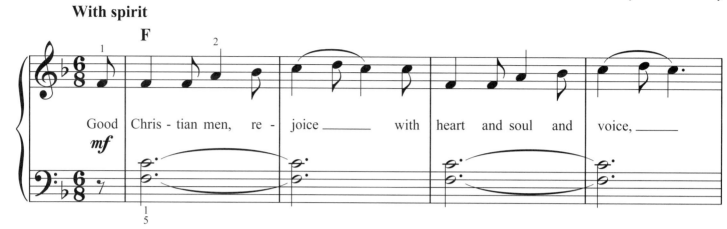

Good Chris - tian men, re - joice _____ with heart and soul and voice, _____

give ye heed to what we say: News! News! Je - sus Christ is

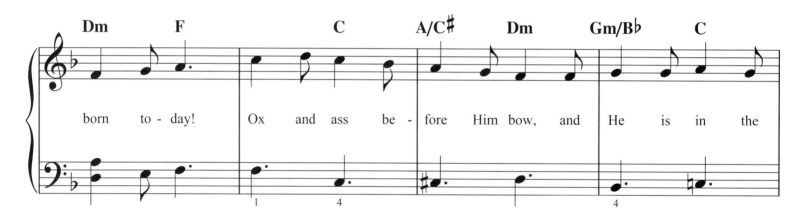

born to - day! Ox and ass be - fore Him bow, and He is in the

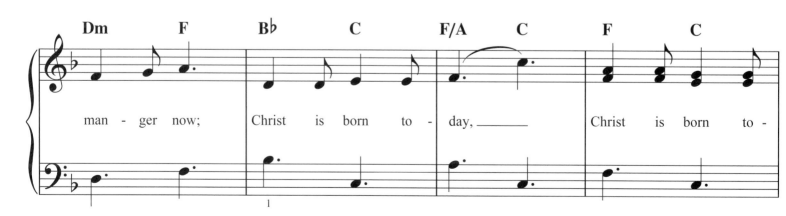

man - ger now; Christ is born to - day, _____ Christ is born to -

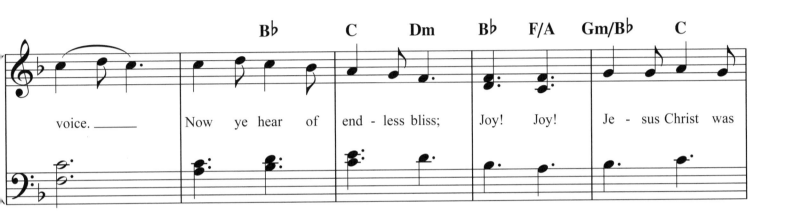

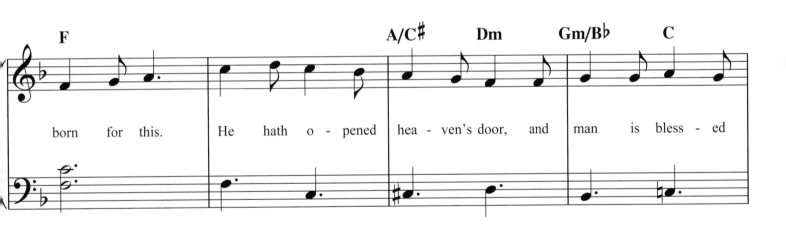

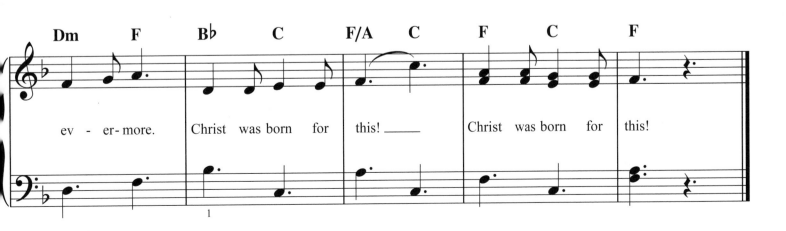

GOOD KING WENCESLAS

Words by JOHN M. NEALE
Music from *Piae Cantiones*

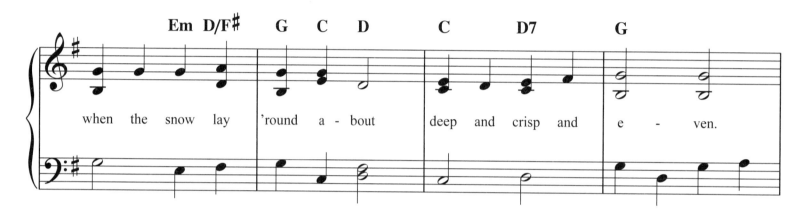

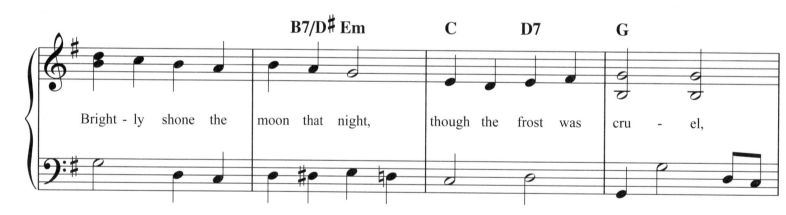

HEAR THEM BELLS

Words and Music by
D.S. McCOSH

HARK! THE HERALD ANGELS SING

Words by CHARLES WESLEY
Altered by GEORGE WHITEFIELD
Music by FELIX MENDELSSOHN-BARTHOLDY
Arranged by WILLIAM H. CUMMINGS

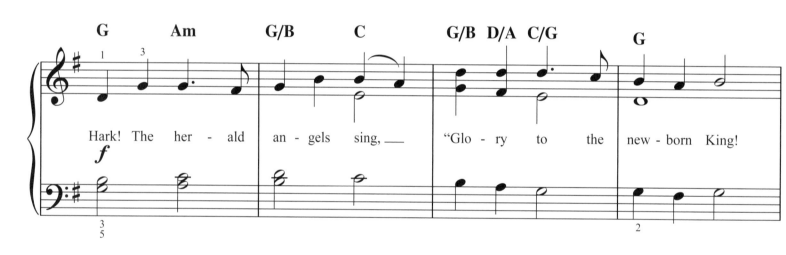

Hark! The her-ald an-gels sing, ___ "Glo-ry to the new-born King!

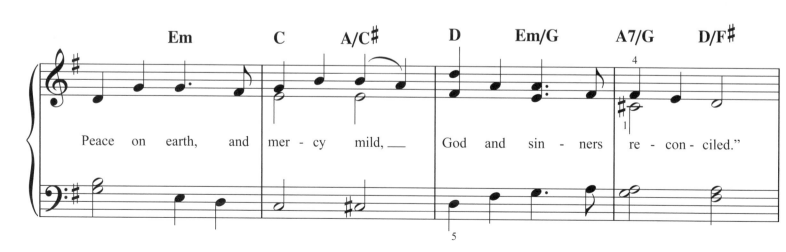

Peace on earth, and mer-cy mild, ___ God and sin-ners re-con-ciled."

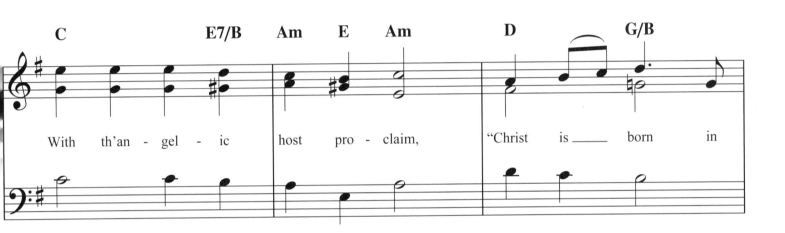

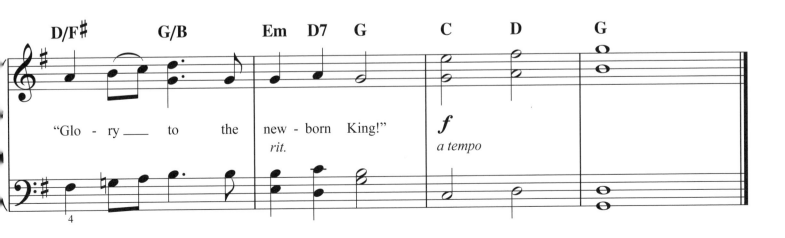

HERE WE COME A-WASSAILING

Traditional

Here we come a - was - sail - ing a -
We're not dai - ly beg - gars that

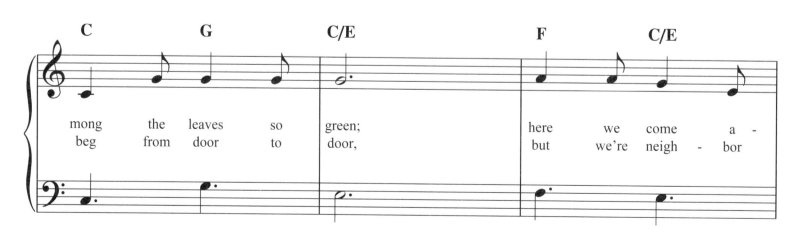

mong the leaves so green;
beg from door to door,

here we come a -
but we're neigh - bor

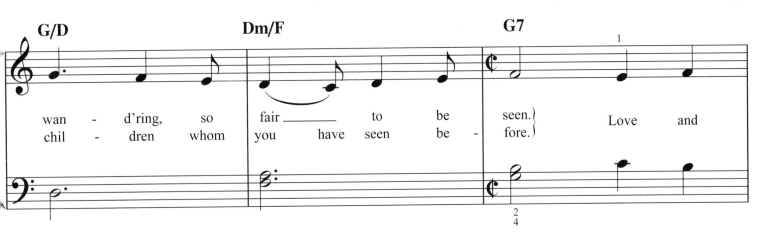

wan - d'ring, so fair _____ to be seen.
chil - dren whom you have seen be - fore.
Love and

joy come to you, and to you your was - sail, too; and God

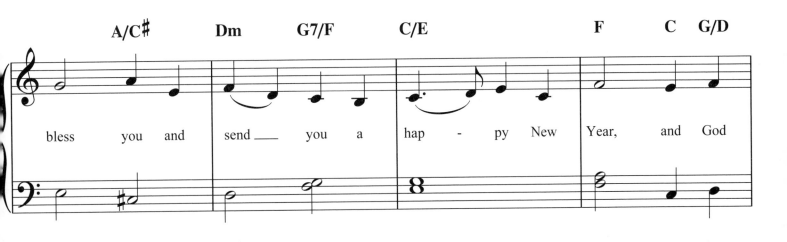

bless you and send _____ you a hap - py New Year, and God

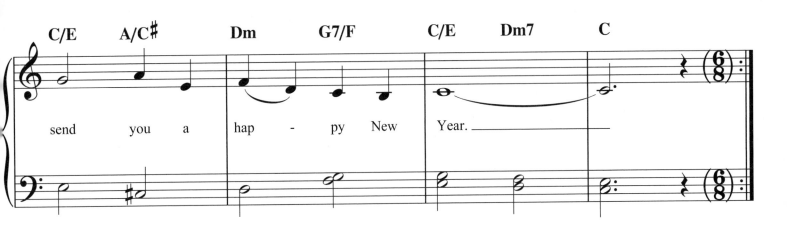

send you a hap - py New Year. _____

THE HOLLY AND THE IVY

18th Century English Carol

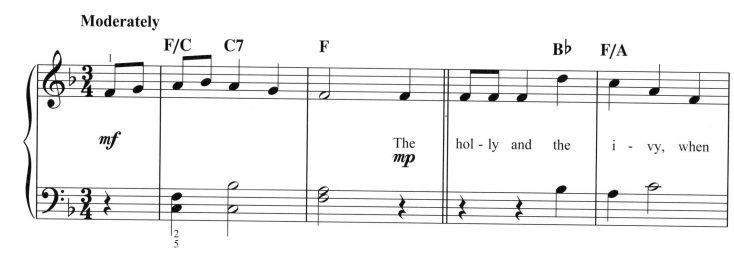

The hol-ly and the i-vy, when

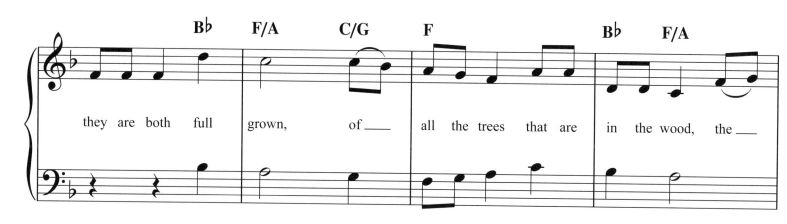

they are both full grown, of __ all the trees that are in the wood, the __

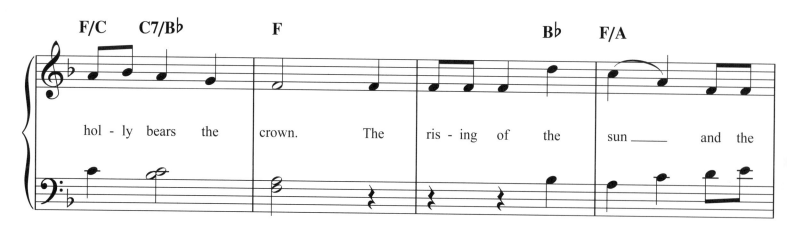

hol-ly bears the crown. The ris-ing of the sun __ and the

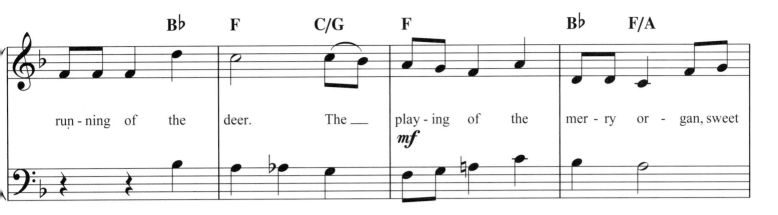

run - ning of the deer. The __ play - ing of the mer - ry or - gan, sweet

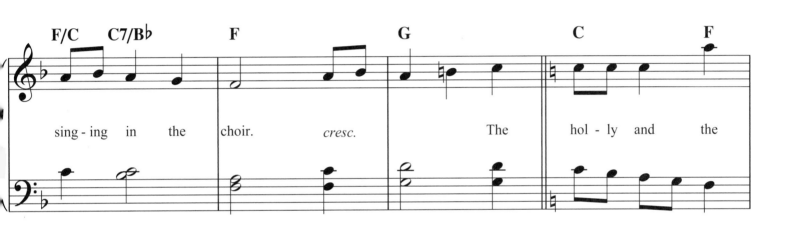

sing - ing in the choir. *cresc.* The hol - ly and the

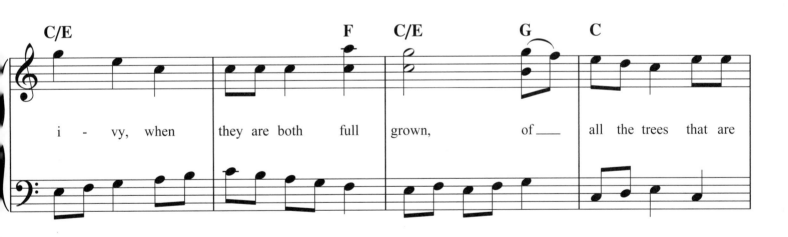

i - vy, when they are both full grown, of __ all the trees that are

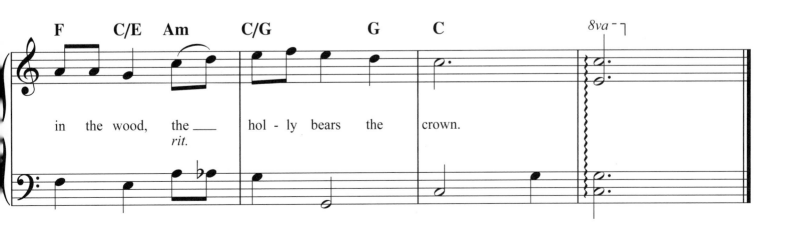

in the wood, the __ hol - ly bears the crown.
rit.

JINGLE BELLS

Words and Music by
J. PIERPONT

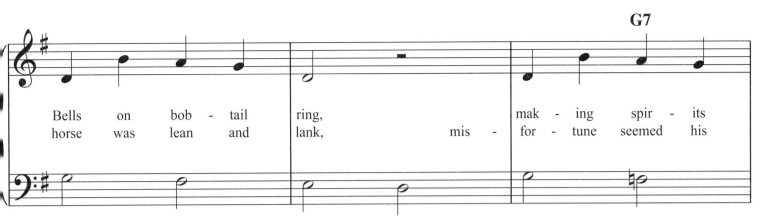

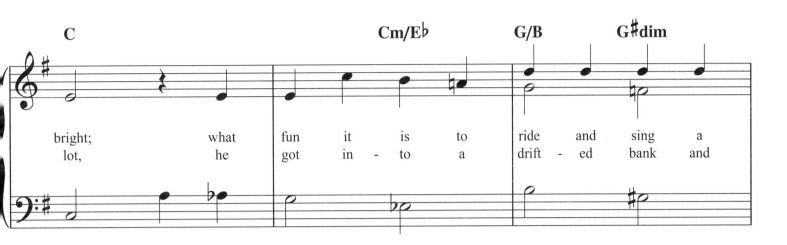

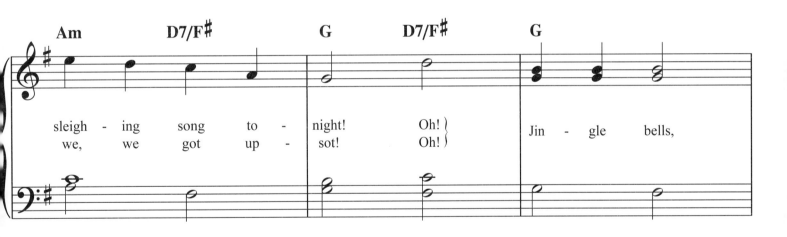

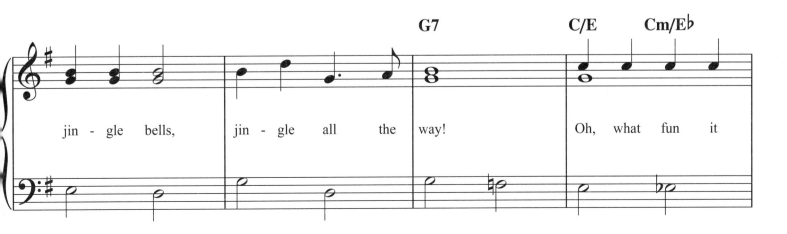

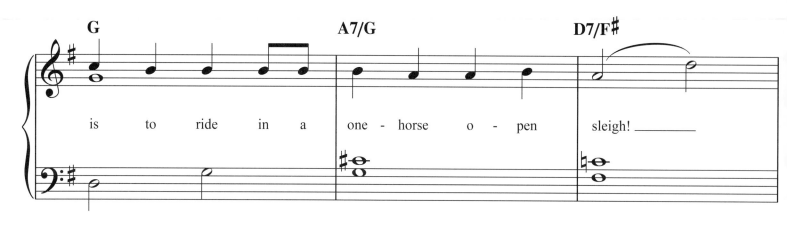

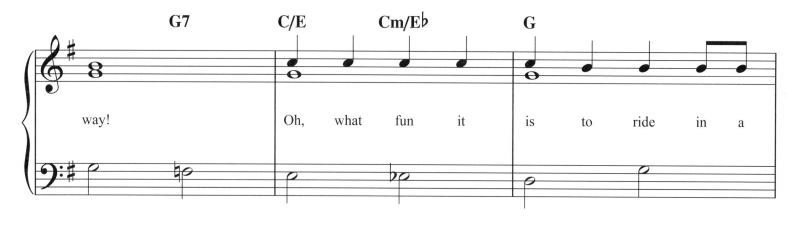

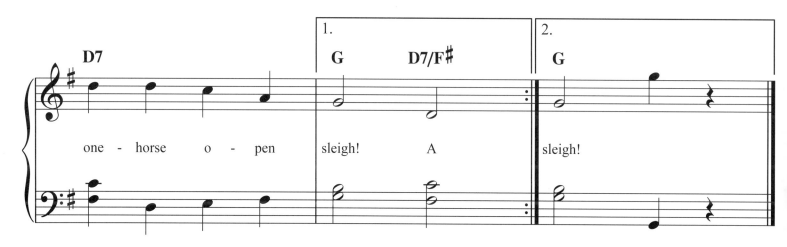

I HEARD THE BELLS ON CHRISTMAS DAY

Words by HENRY WADSWORTH LONGFELLOW
Music by JOHN BAPTISTE CALKIN

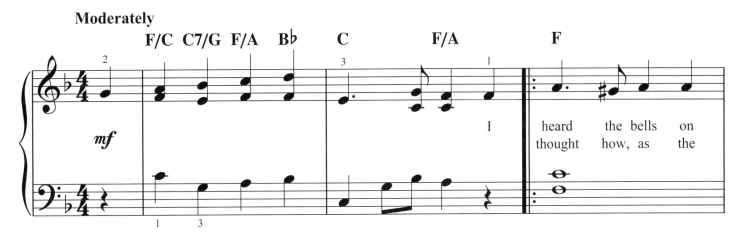

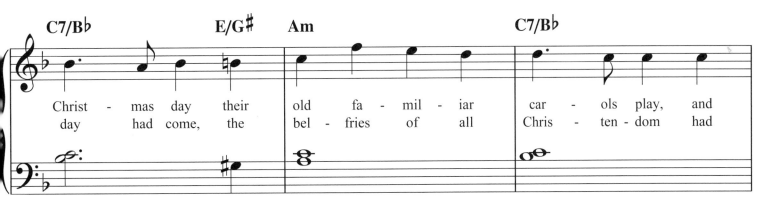

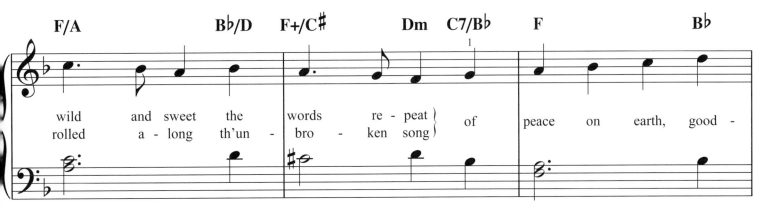

I SAW THREE SHIPS

Traditional English Carol

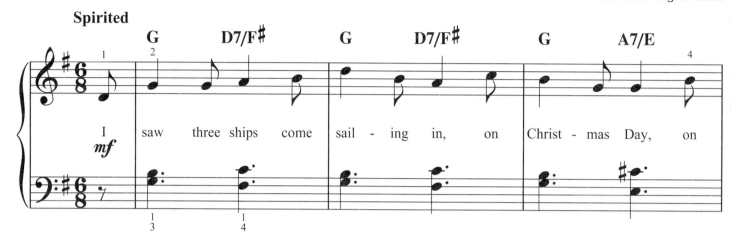

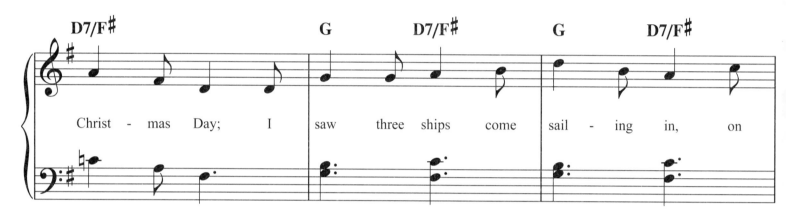

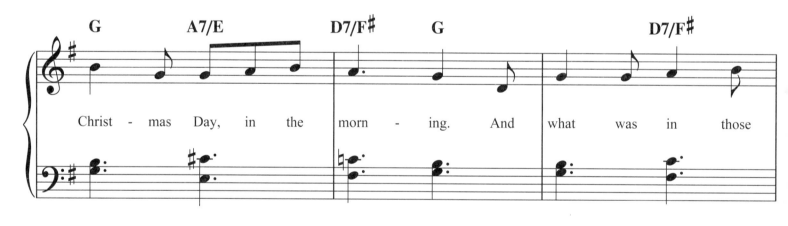

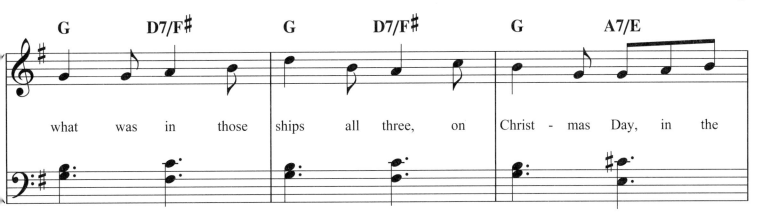

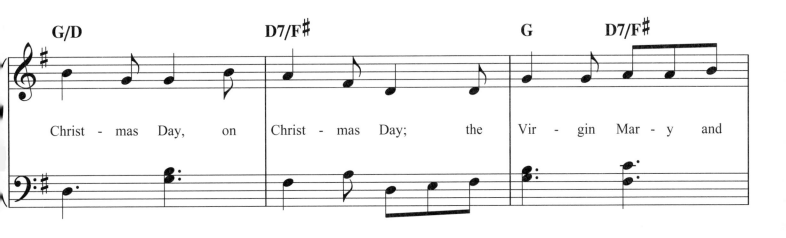

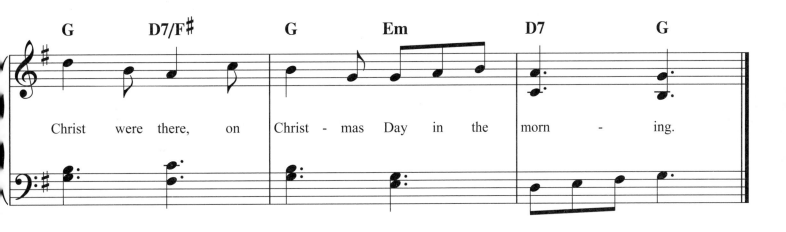

IN THE BLEAK MIDWINTER

Poem by CHRISTINA ROSSETTI
Music by GUSTAV HOLST

Moderately slow

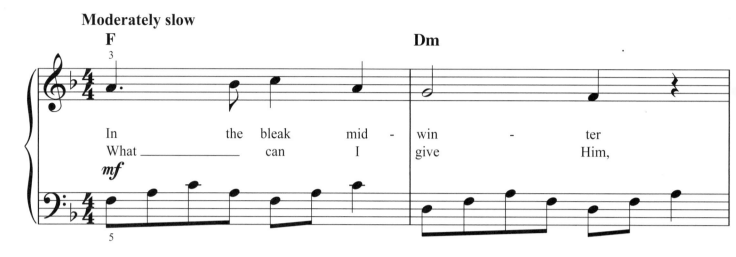

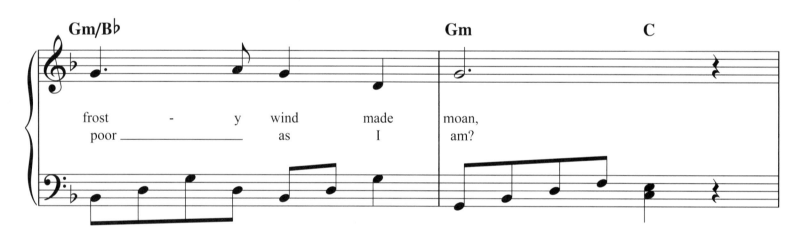

IT CAME UPON THE MIDNIGHT CLEAR

Words by EDMUND HAMILTON SEARS
Music by RICHARD STORRS WILLIS

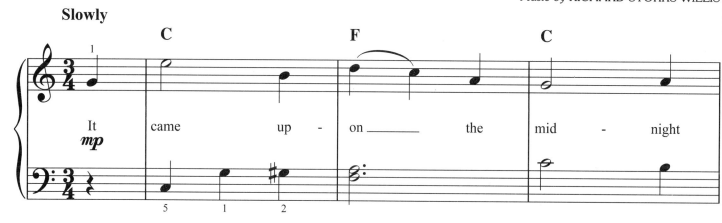

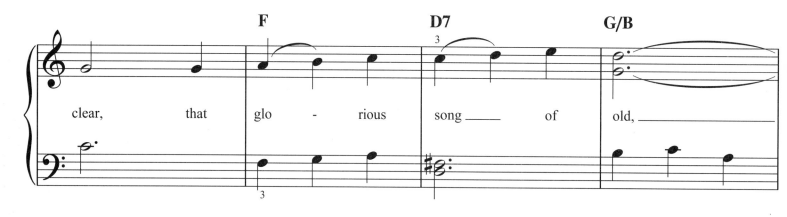

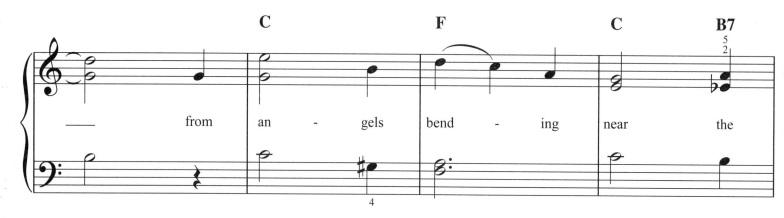

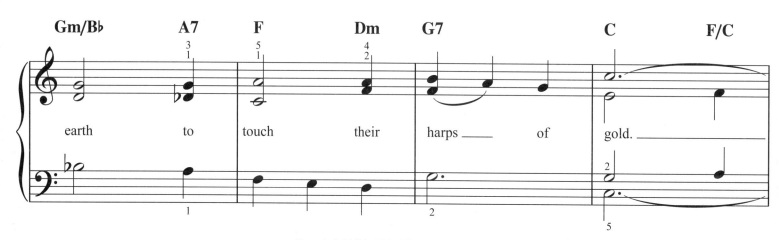

Peace on the earth _____ good - will to

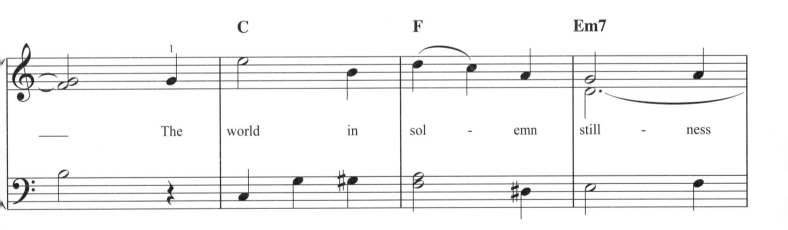

men, from heaven's ___ all - gra - cious King. _____

_____ The world in sol - emn still - ness

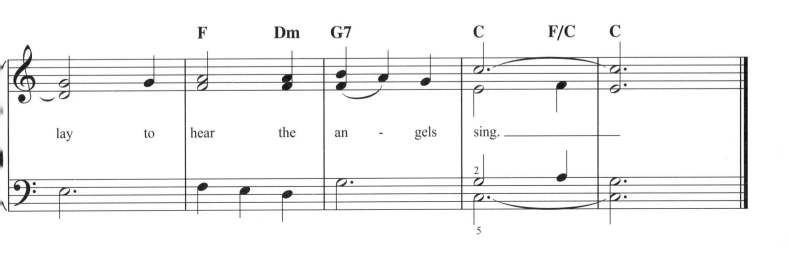

lay to hear the an - gels sing. _____

MARCH
from THE NUTCRACKER

By PYOTR IL'YICH TCHAIKOVSKY

Moderately, in 2

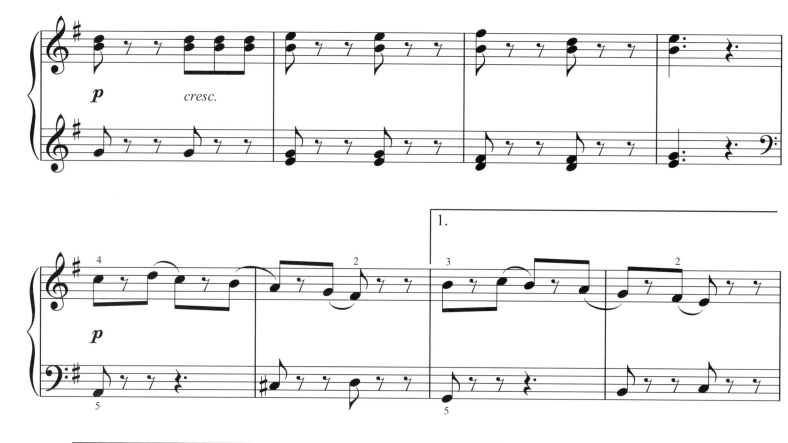

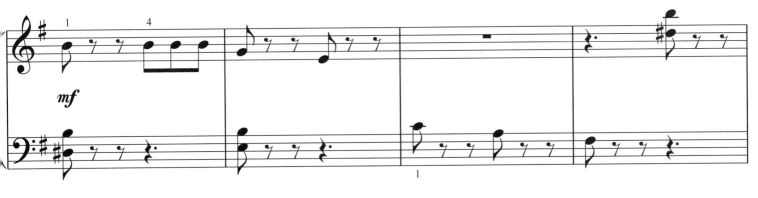

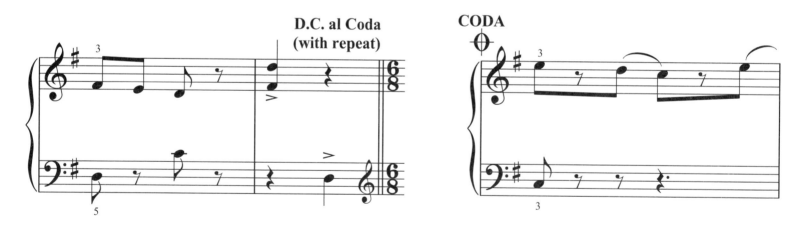

JOLLY OLD ST. NICHOLAS

Traditional 19th Century American Carol

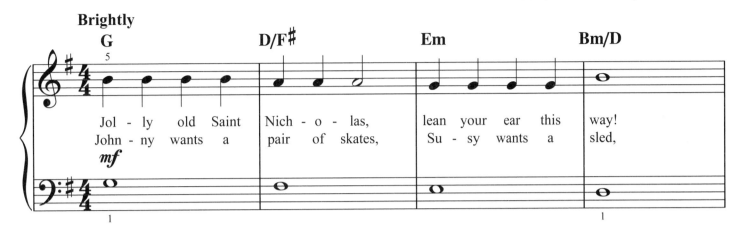

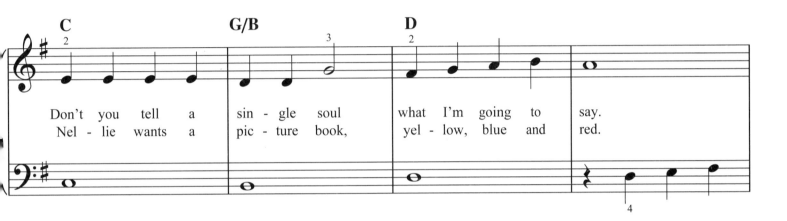

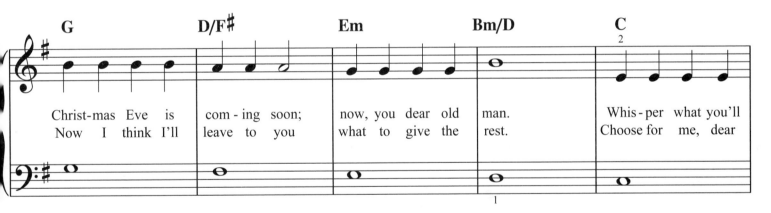

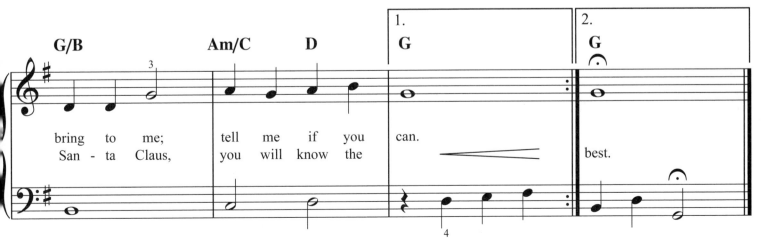

JOY TO THE WORLD

Words by ISAAC WATTS
Music by GEORGE FRIDERIC HANDEL
Adapted by LOWELL MASON

heart _____ pre - pare ___ Him ___ room, _____ and
of _____ His right - eous - ness, _____ and

heav'n and na - ture ___ sing, and ___ heav'n and na - ture ___
won - ders of His ___ love, and ___ won - ders of His ___

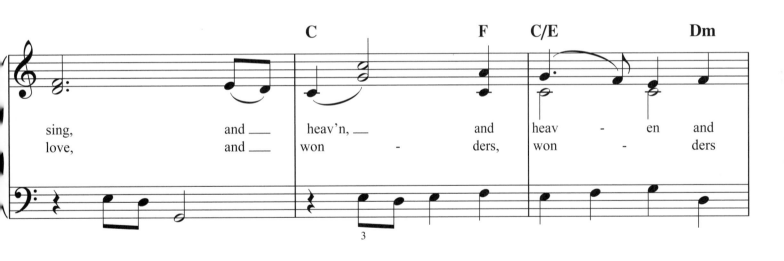

sing, and ___ heav'n, ___ and heav - en and
love, and ___ won - ders, won - ders

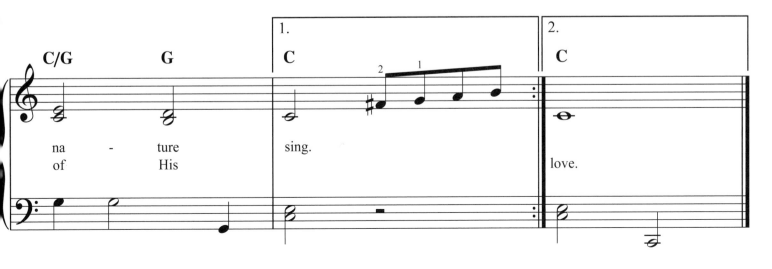

na - ture sing.
of His love.

O CHRISTMAS TREE

Traditional German Carol

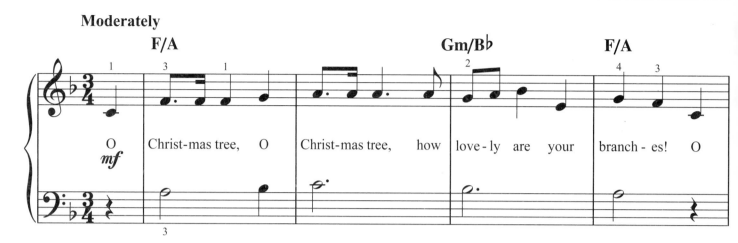

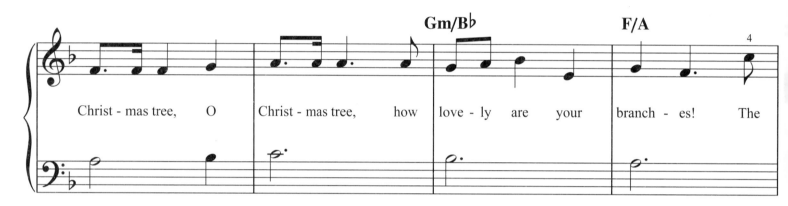

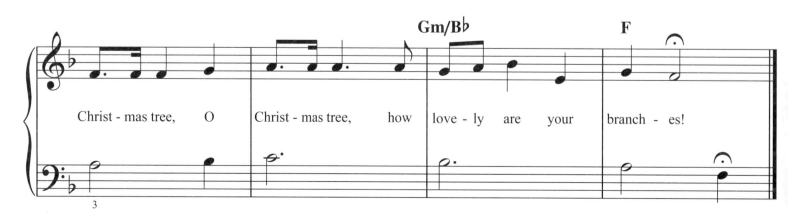

ONCE IN ROYAL DAVID'S CITY

Words by CECIL F. ALEXANDER
Music by HENRY J. GAUNTLETT

O COME, ALL YE FAITHFUL
(Adeste Fideles)

Music by JOHN FRANCIS WADE
Latin Words translated by FREDERICK OAKELEY

Triumphantly

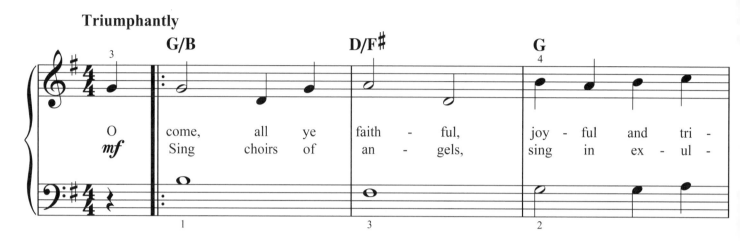

O come, all ye faith - ful,
joy - ful and tri -
Sing choirs of an - gels,
sing in ex - ul -

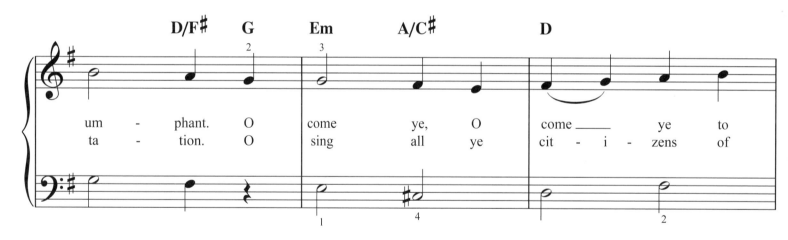

um - phant. O come ye, O come _____ ye to
ta - tion. O sing all ye cit - i - zens of

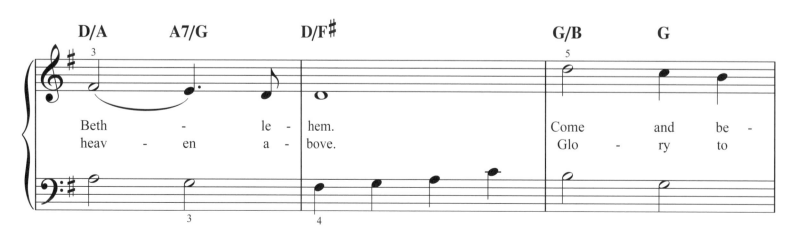

Beth - le - hem.
Come and be -
heav - en a - bove.
Glo - ry to

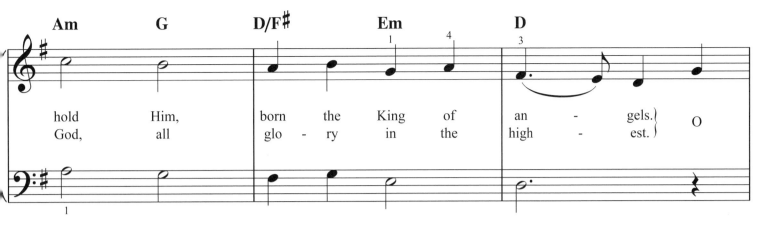

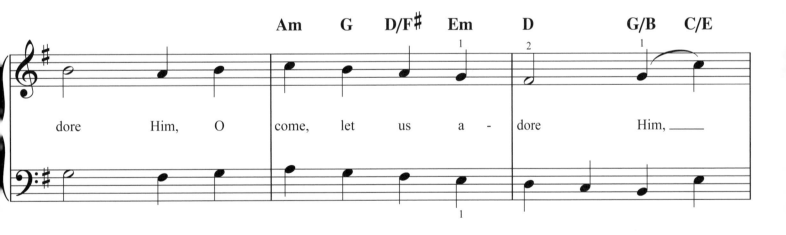

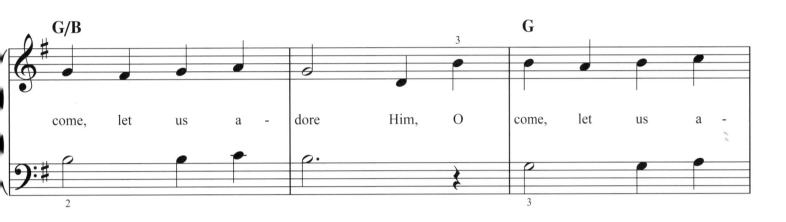

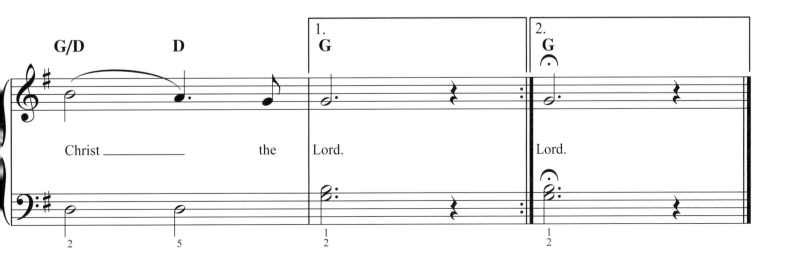

O COME, O COME IMMANUEL

Plainsong, 13th Century
Words translated by JOHN M. NEALE
and HENRY S. COFFIN

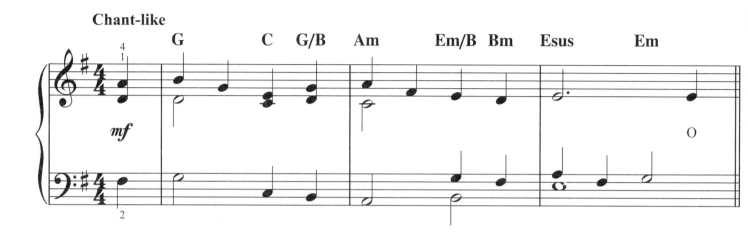

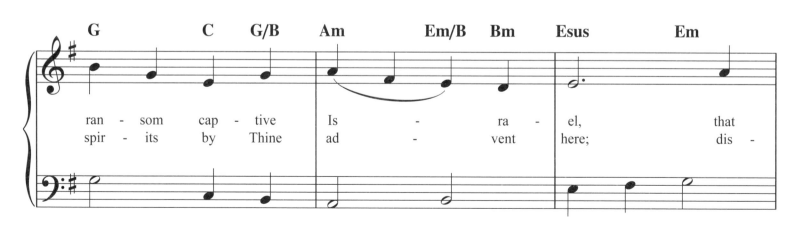

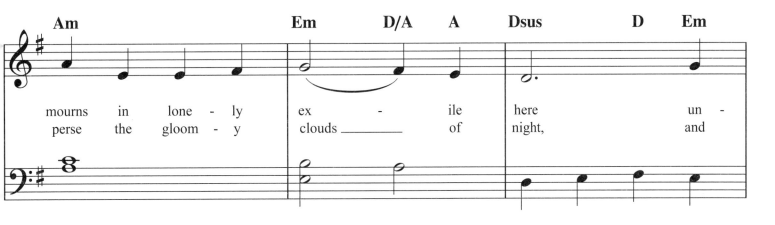

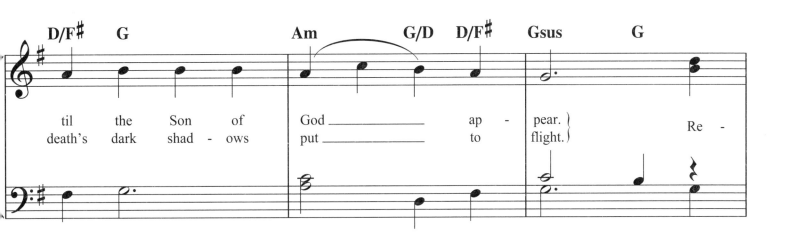

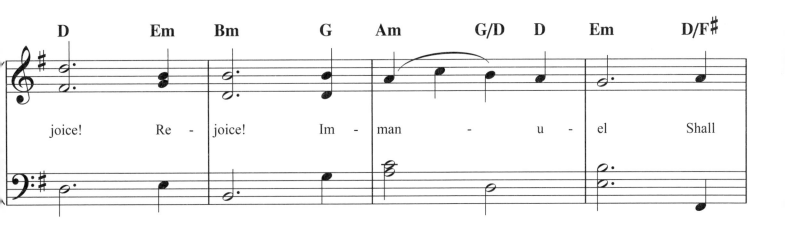

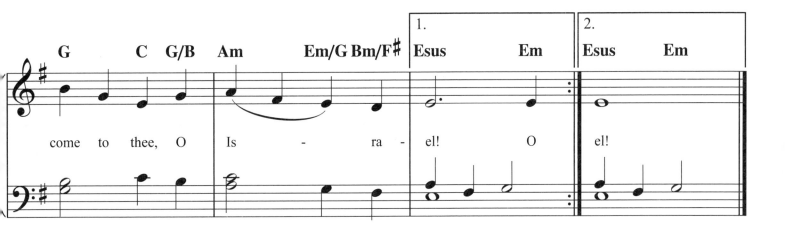

O HOLY NIGHT

French Words by PLACIDE CAPPEAU
English Words by JOHN S. DWIGHT
Music by ADOLPHE ADAM

Flowing

O ho - ly
Tru - ly He

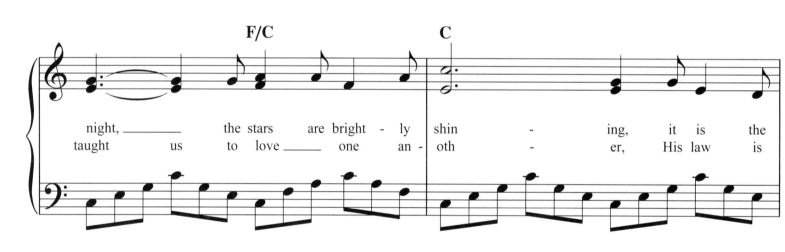

night, _____ the stars are bright - ly shin - ing, it is the
taught us to love _____ one an - oth - er, His law is

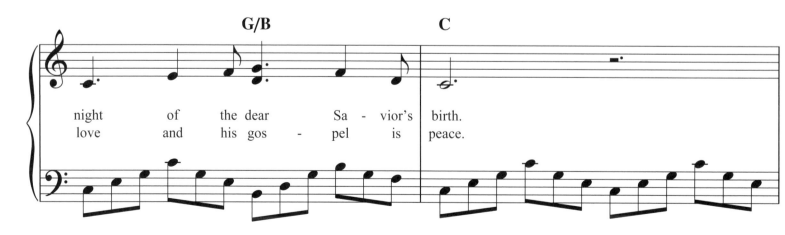

night of the dear Sa - vior's birth.
love and his gos - pel is peace.

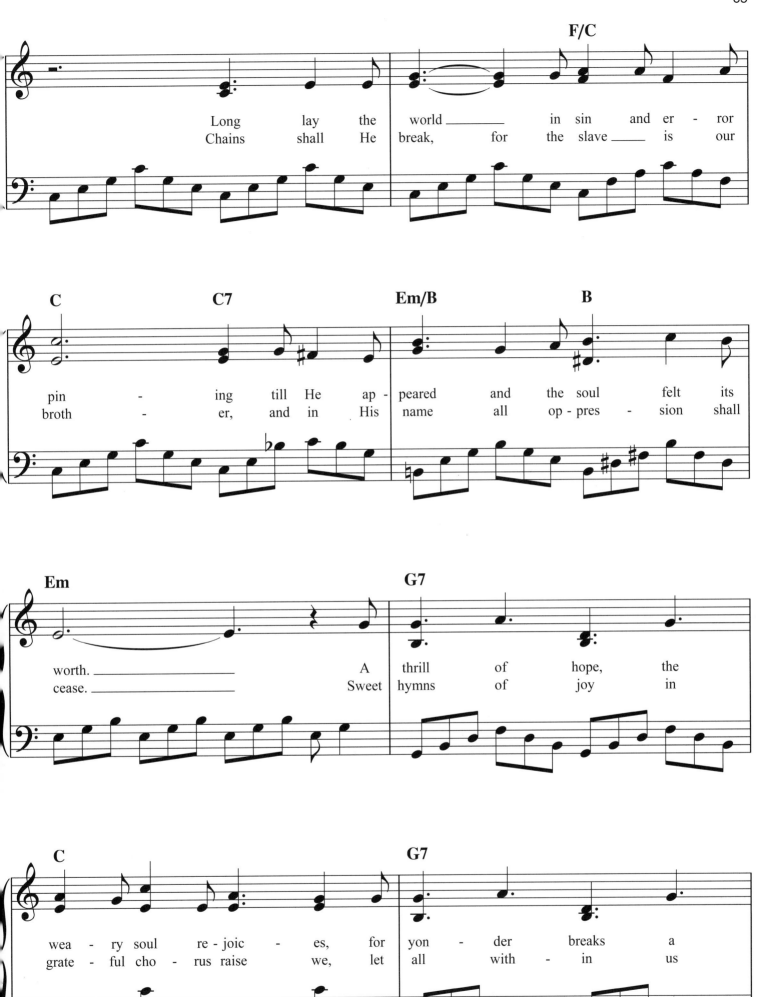

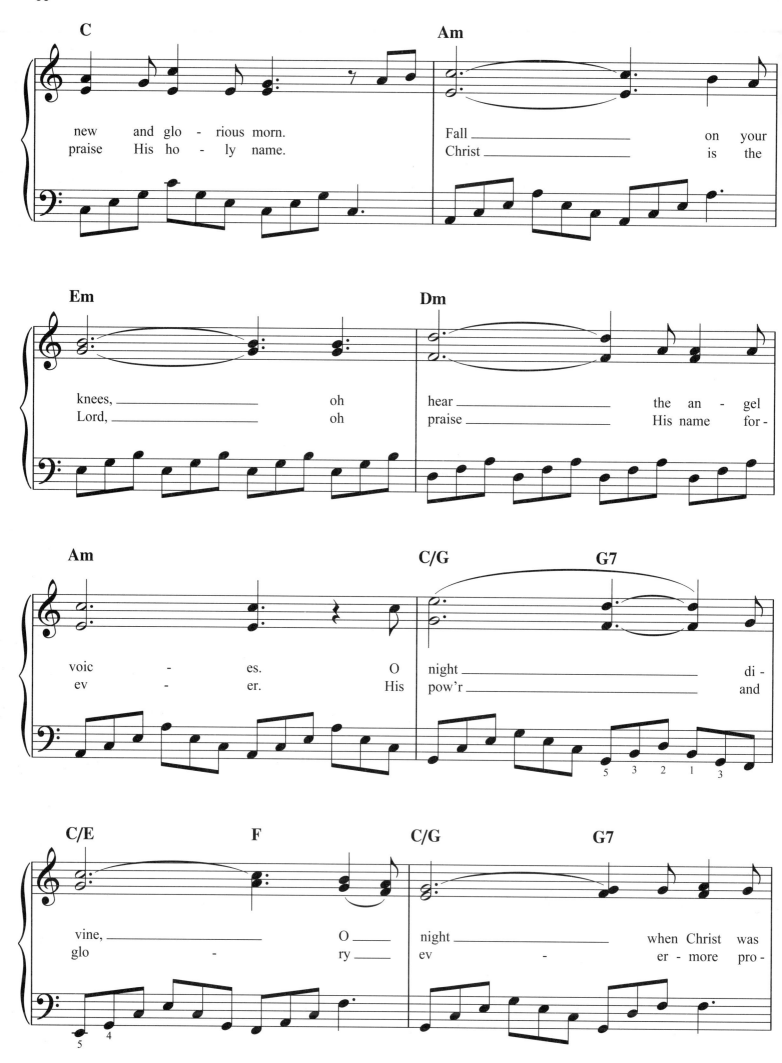

O LITTLE TOWN OF BETHLEHEM

Words by PHILLIPS BROOKS
Music by LEWIS H. REDNER

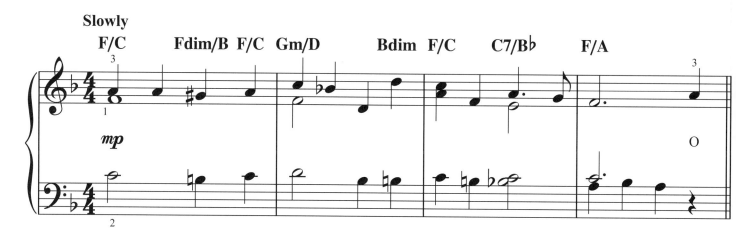

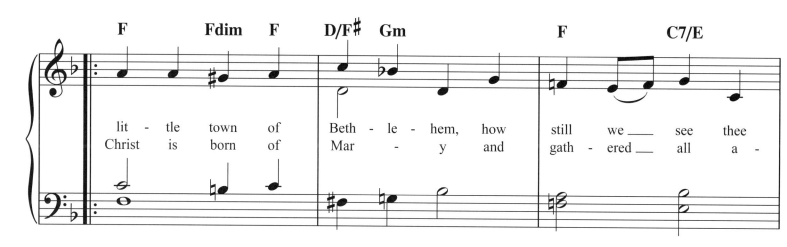

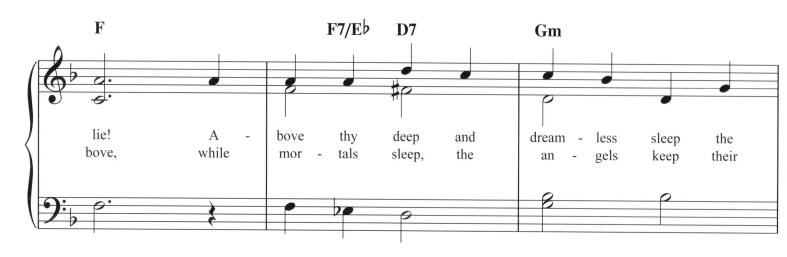

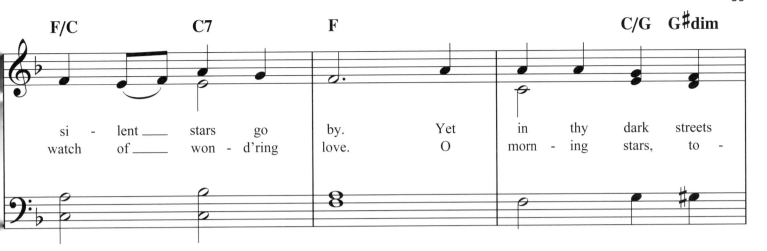

si - lent ___ stars go by. Yet in thy dark streets
watch of ___ won - d'ring love. O morn - ing stars, to -

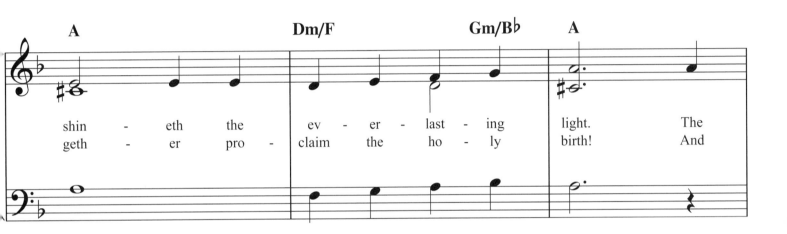

shin - eth the ev - er - last - ing light. The
geth - er pro - claim the ho - ly birth! And

hopes and fears of all the years are met in thee to -
prais - es sing to God the King, and peace to all on

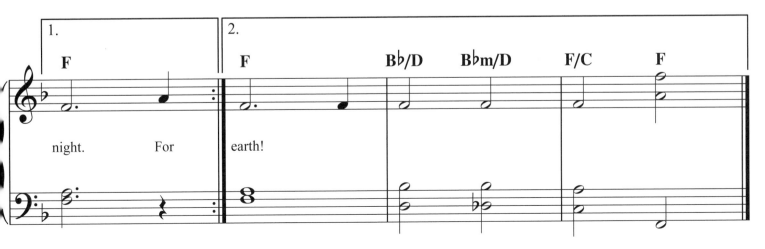

1.
night. For

2.
earth!

SILENT NIGHT

Words by JOSEPH MOHR
Translated by JOHN F. YOUNG
Music by FRANZ X. GRUBER

Si - lent night, ho - ly
Si - lent night, ho - ly

night! All is calm, all is
night! Shep - herds quake at the

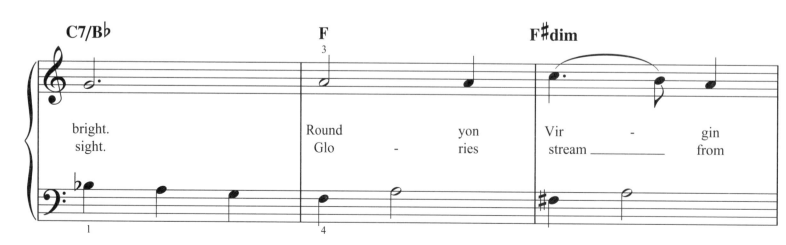

bright. Round yon Vir - gin
sight. Glo - ries stream _____ from

SIMPLE GIFTS

Traditional Shaker Hymn

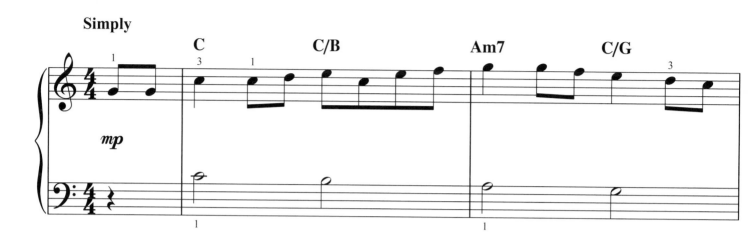

'Tis the gift to be sim-ple, 'tis the

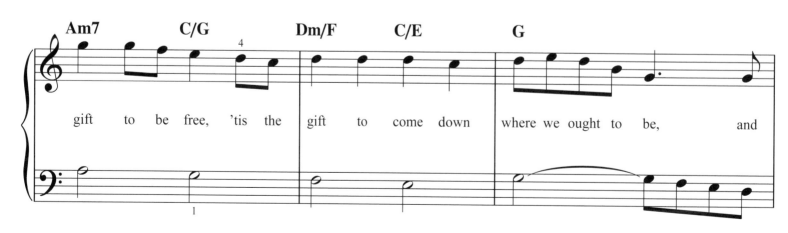

gift to be free, 'tis the gift to come down where we ought to be, and

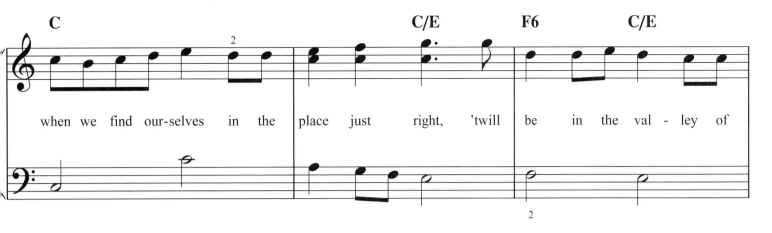

when we find our-selves in the place just right, 'twill be in the val - ley of

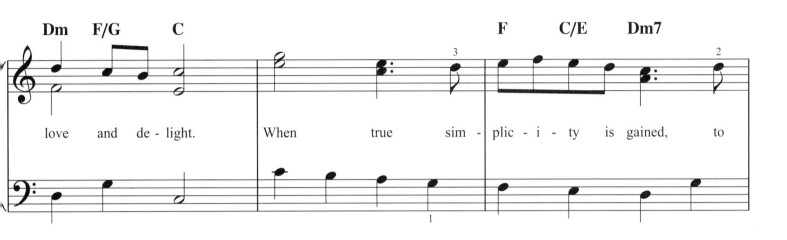

love and de - light. When true sim - plic - i - ty is gained, to

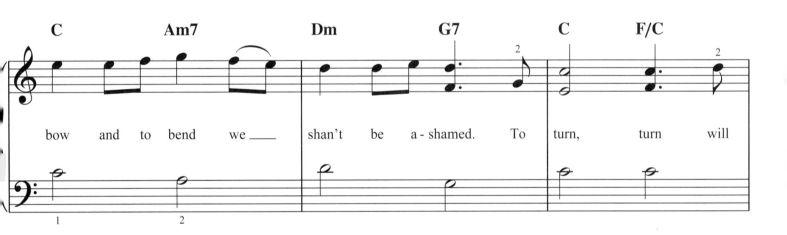

bow and to bend we ___ shan't be a - shamed. To turn, turn will

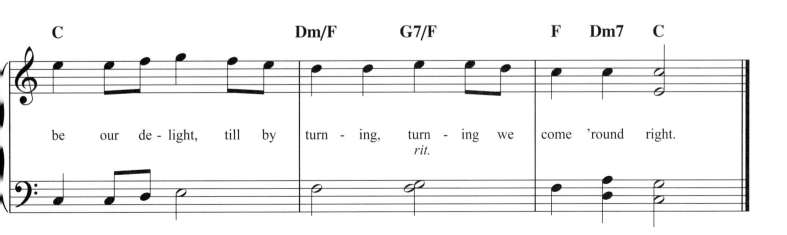

be our de - light, till by turn - ing, turn - ing we come 'round right.
rit.

UP ON THE HOUSETOP

Words and Music by
B.R. HANBY

STAR OF THE EAST

Words by GEORGE COOPER
Music by AMANDA KENNEDY

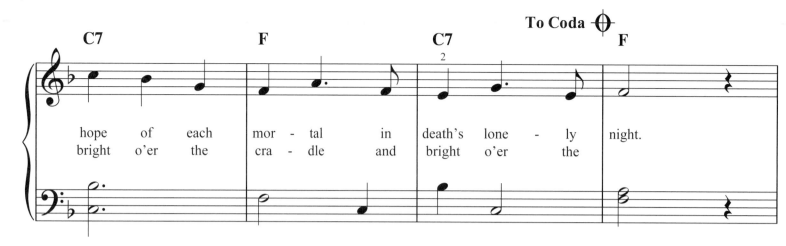

To Coda

hope of each mor - tal in death's lone - ly night.
bright o'er each the cra - dle and bright o'er the

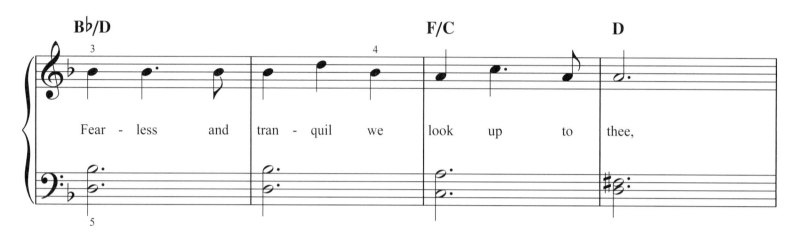

Fear - less and tran - quil we look up to thee,

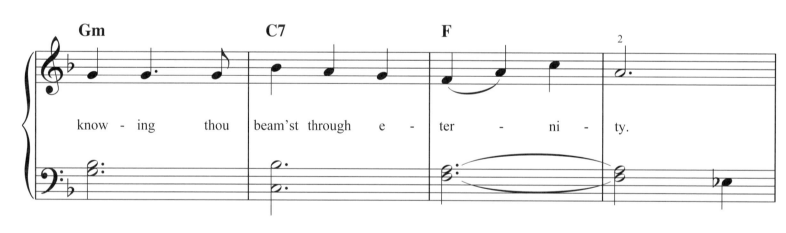

know - ing thou beam'st through e - ter - ni - ty.

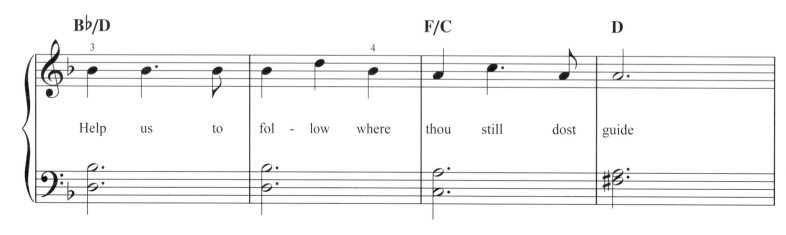

Help us to fol - low where thou still dost guide

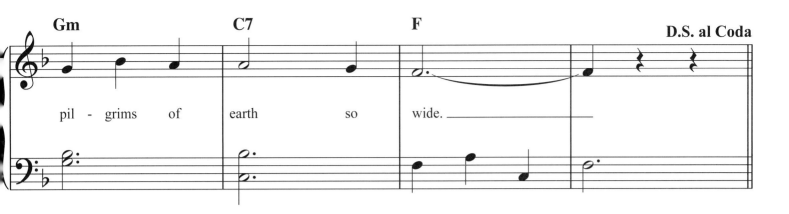

Gm **C7** **F** **D.S. al Coda**

pil - grims of earth so wide. _____

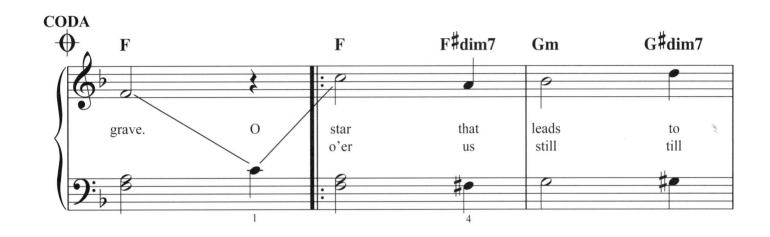

CODA

F **F** **F♯dim7** **Gm** **G♯dim7**

grave. O star that leads to
o'er us still till

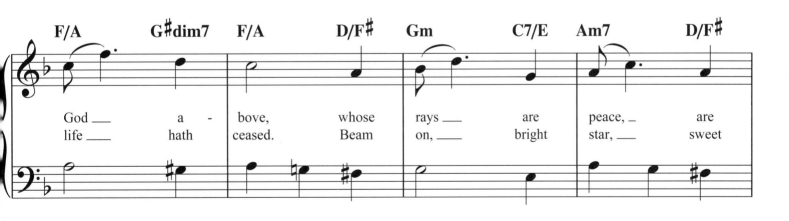

F/A **G♯dim7** **F/A** **D/F♯** **Gm** **C7/E** **Am7** **D/F♯**

God ___ a - bove, whose rays ___ are peace, __ are
life ___ a hath ceased. Beam on, ___ bright star, ___ sweet

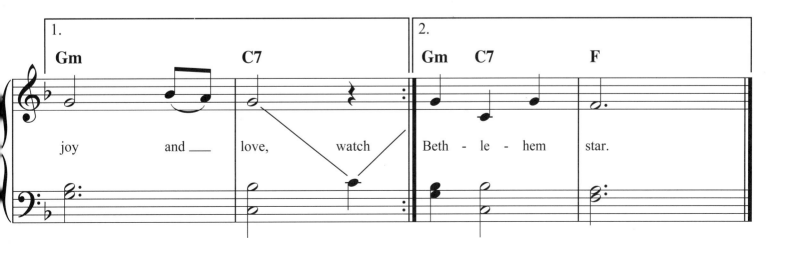

1.
Gm **C7**

2.
Gm **C7** **F**

joy and ___ love, watch Beth - le - hem star.

STILL, STILL, STILL

Salzburg Melody, c.1819
Traditional Austrian Text

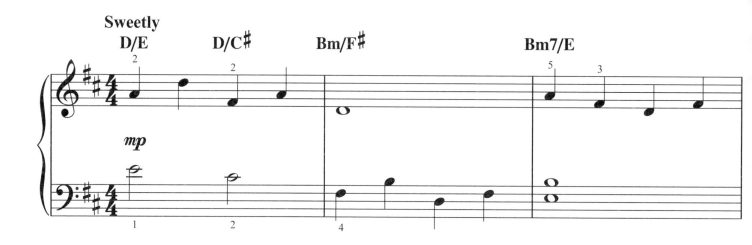

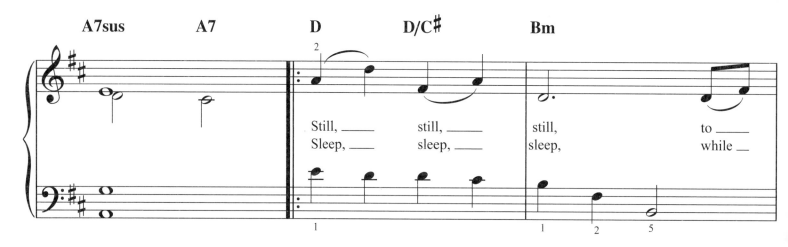

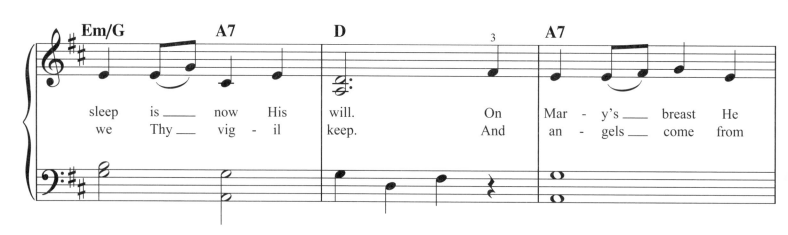

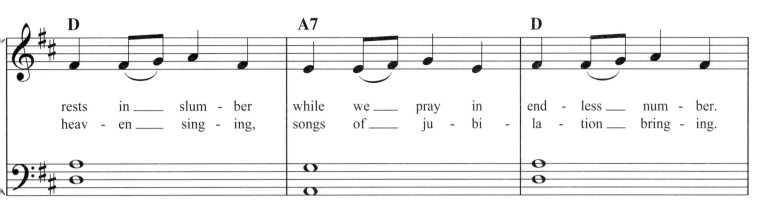

rests in ___ slum - ber   while we ___ pray in   end - less ___ num - ber.
heav - en ___ sing - ing,   songs of ___ ju - bi - la - tion ___ bring - ing.

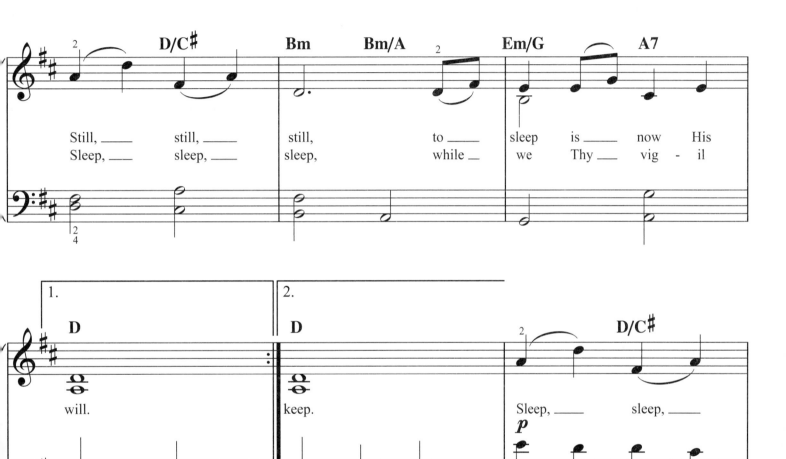

Still, ___ still, ___   still,   to ___ sleep is ___ now His
Sleep, ___ sleep, ___   sleep,   while __ we Thy ___ vig - il

1. will.
2. keep.

Sleep, ___ sleep, ___

p

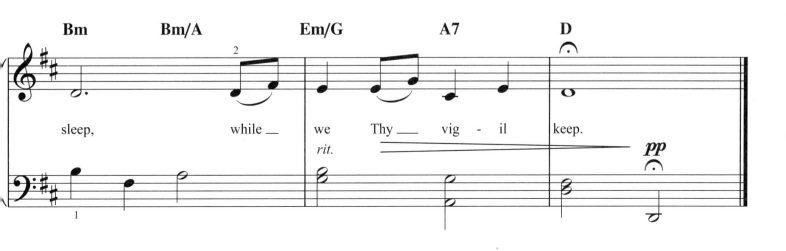

sleep,   while __ we Thy ___ vig - il keep.

rit.   *pp*

SUSSEX CAROL

Traditional English Carol

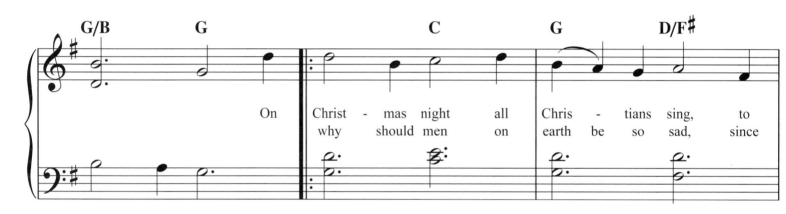

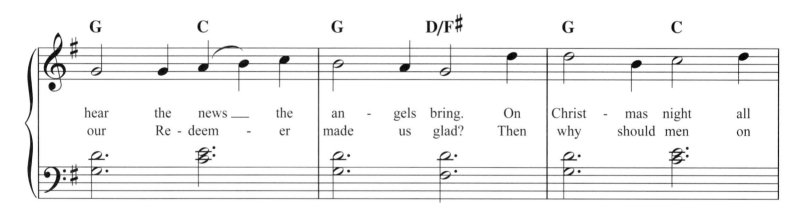

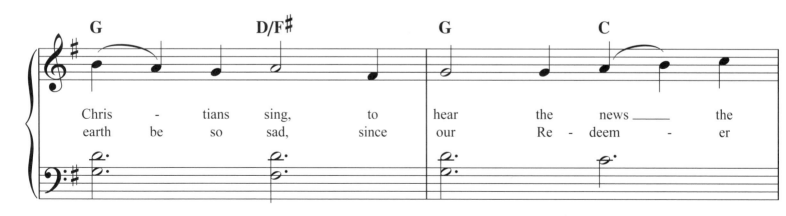

THE TWELVE DAYS OF CHRISTMAS

Traditional English Carol

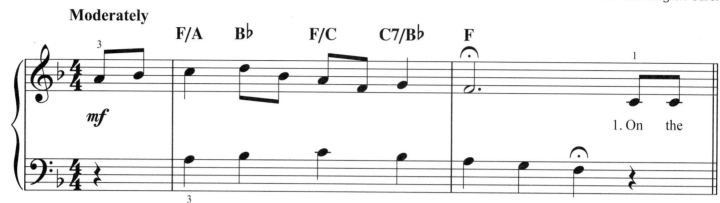

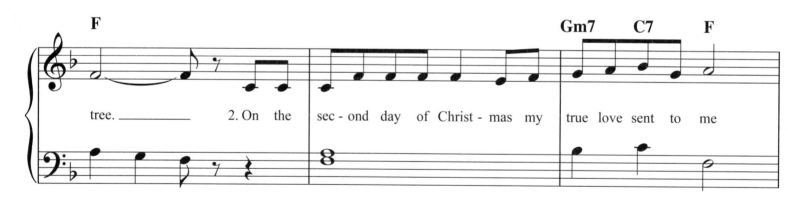

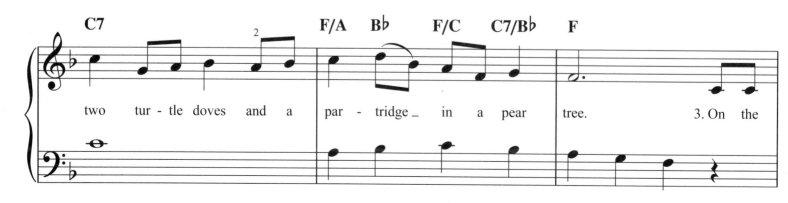

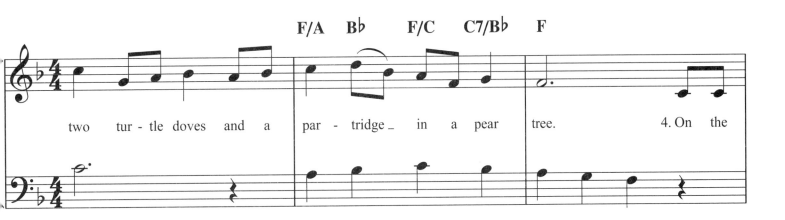

F   **Gm7/B♭**   **C7**   **F**

tree.   5. On   the   fifth   day   of   Christ - mas   my   true love sent to me

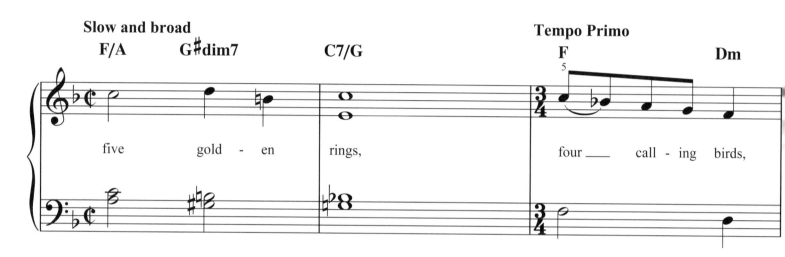

Slow and broad   **Tempo Primo**

F/A   **G♯dim7**   **C7/G**   **F**   **Dm**

five   gold - en   rings,   four ___ call - ing birds,

B♭   **C7**   **F/A** **B♭**   **F/C**   **C7/B♭**

three French hens,   two ___ tur - tle doves   and   a   par - tridge ___ in   a   pear

F   **Gm7/B♭**   **C7**   **F**

tree.   6. On   the   sixth   day   of   Christ - mas   my   true love sent to me

7.-12. (See additional verses)

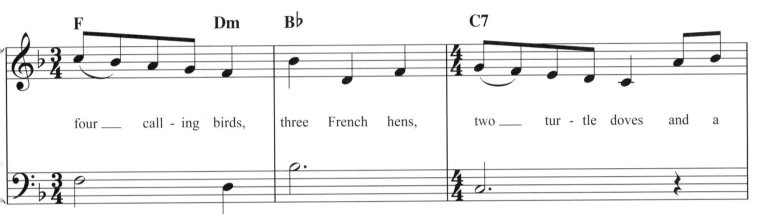

Additional Verses

Seven swans a-swimming
Eight maids a-milking
Nine ladies dancing
Ten lords a-leaping
Eleven pipers piping
Twelve drummers drumming

WE THREE KINGS OF ORIENT ARE

Words and Music by
JOHN H. HOPKINS, JR.

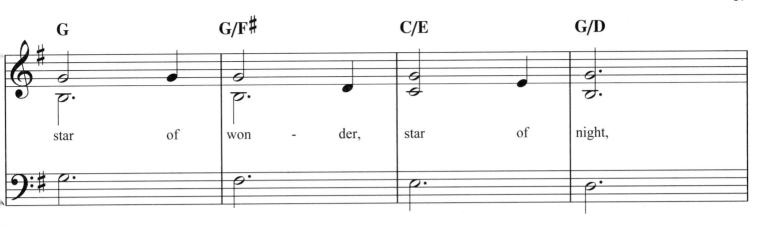

star of won - der, star of night,

star with roy - al beau - ty bright,

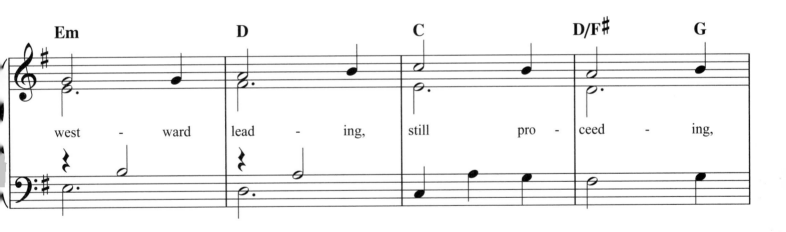

west - ward lead - ing, still pro - ceed - ing,

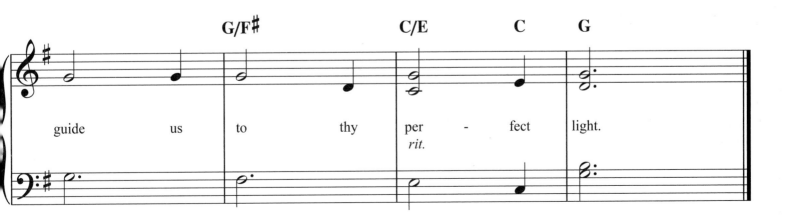

guide us to thy per - fect light.
rit.

WE WISH YOU A MERRY CHRISTMAS

Traditional English Folksong

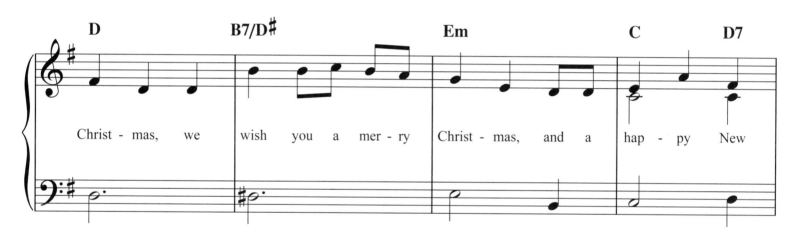

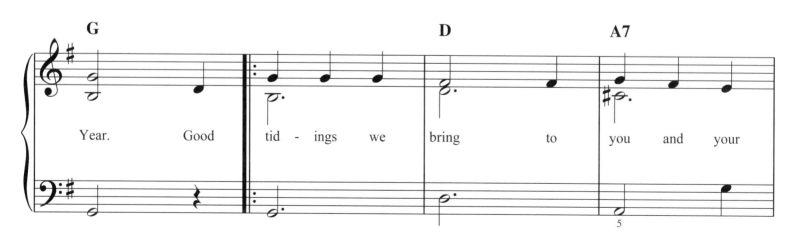

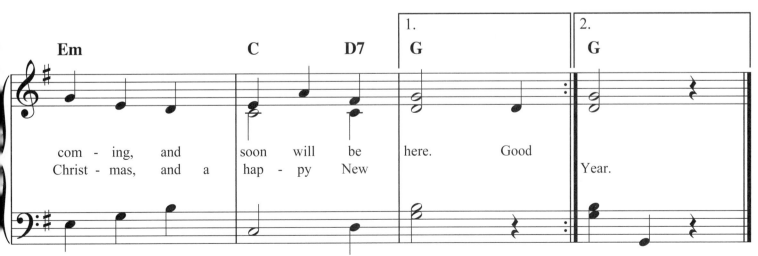

WHAT CHILD IS THIS?

Words by WILLIAM C. DIX
16th Century English Melody

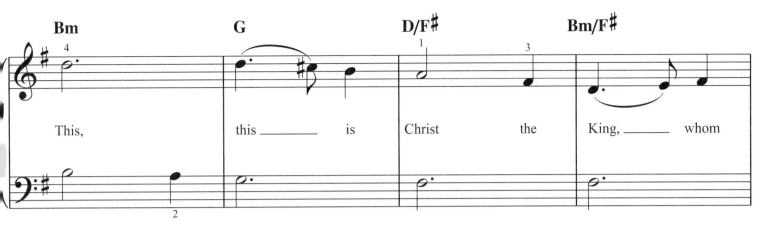

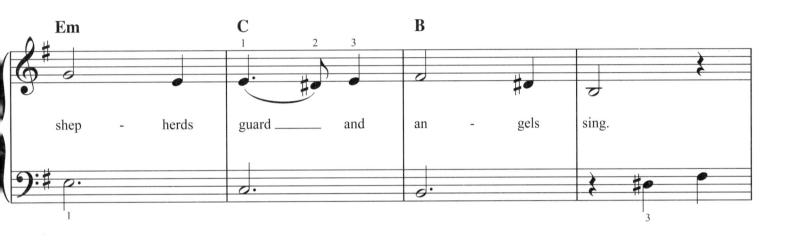

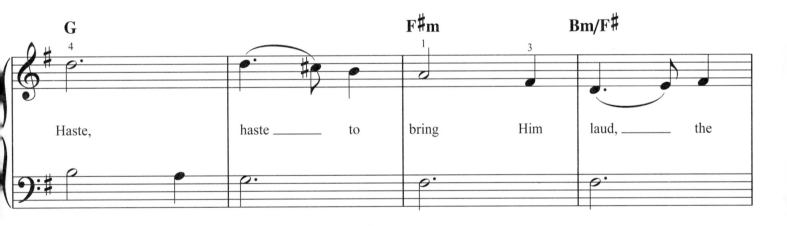

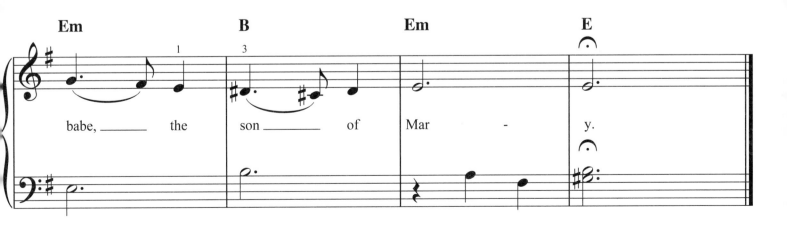

UKRAINIAN BELL CAROL

Traditional
Arranged by MYKOLA LEONTOVYCH

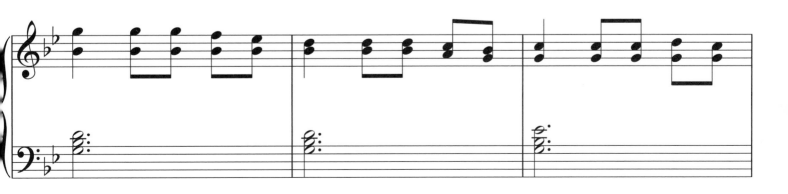

WHILE SHEPHERDS WATCHED THEIR FLOCKS

Words by NAHUM TATE
Music by GEORGE FRIDERIC HANDEL

EASY PIANO PLAY-ALONGS
Orchestrated arrangements with you as the soloist!

This series lets you play along with great accompaniments to songs you know and love! Each book comes with recordings of complete professional performances and includes matching custom arrangements in easy piano format. With these books you can: Listen to complete professional performances of each of the songs; Play the easy piano arrangements along with the performances; Sing along with the recordings; Play the easy piano arrangements as solos, without the audio.

1. GREAT JAZZ STANDARDS
00310916 Book/CD Pack...$14.95

2. FAVORITE CLASSICAL THEMES
00310921 Book/CD Pack...$14.95

3. BROADWAY FAVORITES
00310915 Book/CD Pack...$14.95

4. ADELE
00156223 Book/Online Audio...............................$16.99

5. HIT POP/ROCK BALLADS
00310917 Book/CD Pack...$14.95

6. LOVE SONG FAVORITES
00310918 Book/CD Pack...$14.95

7. O HOLY NIGHT
00310920 Book/CD Pack...$14.95

9. COUNTRY BALLADS
00311105 Book/CD Pack...$14.95

11. DISNEY BLOCKBUSTERS
00311107 Book/Online Audio...............................$14.99

12. CHRISTMAS FAVORITES
00311257 Book/CD Pack...$14.95

13. CHILDREN'S SONGS
00311258 Book/CD Pack...$14.95

15. DISNEY'S BEST
00311260 Book/Online Audio..............................$16.99

16. LENNON & McCARTNEY HITS
00311262 Book/CD Pack...$14.95

17. HOLIDAY HITS
00311329 Book/CD Pack...$14.95

18. WEST SIDE STORY
00130739 Book/Online Audio $14.99

19. TAYLOR SWIFT
00142735 Book/Online Audio $14.99

20. ANDREW LLOYD WEBBER – FAVORITES
00311775 Book/CD Pack...$14.99

21. GREAT CLASSICAL MELODIES
00311776 Book/CD Pack...$14.99

22. ANDREW LLOYD WEBBER – HITS
00311785 Book/CD Pack...$14.99

23. DISNEY CLASSICS
00311836 Book/CD Pack...$14.99

24. LENNON & McCARTNEY FAVORITES
00311837 Book/CD Pack...$14.99

26. WICKED
00311882 Book/CD Pack...$16.99

27. THE SOUND OF MUSIC
00311897 Book/Online Audio..............................$14.99

28. CHRISTMAS CAROLS
00311912 Book/CD Pack...$14.99

29. CHARLIE BROWN CHRISTMAS
00311913 Book/CD Pack...$14.99

31. STAR WARS
00110283 Book/Online Audio $16.99

32. SONGS FROM FROZEN, TANGLED AND ENCHANTED
00126896 Book/Online Audio $14.99

Disney characters and artwork © Disney Enterprises, Inc.

Prices, contents and availability subject to change without notice.

FOR MORE INFORMATION, SEE YOUR LOCAL MUSIC DEALER, OR WRITE TO:

HAL•LEONARD®
CORPORATION
7777 W. BLUEMOUND RD. P.O. BOX 13819 MILWAUKEE, WI 53213

www.halleonard.com

0516